BEST VACATION EVER

THE ULTIMATE TRAVEL GUIDE
RENEW • RECHARGE • RECONNECT

THOR CHALLGREN

Copyright © 2022 by Thor Challgren

All rights reserved.

Published by Flying Lessons Press

No portion of this book may be reproduced in any form without written permission from the publisher or author, except as permitted by U.S. copyright law.

Print ISBN: 979-8-9862342-0-5
ebook ISBN: 979-8-9862342-1-2

052022

FOR MOM AND DAD

Who instilled in me a love of travel and discovery.

Contents

GET THE MOST FROM THIS BOOK	1
INTRODUCTION	3
PART 1 - ON VACATION	15
1. MAKE GRATITUDE YOUR SUPERPOWER	17
2. THE POWER OF THE NOW VACATION	39
3. PAMPER YOUR WELL-BEING	55
4. NURTURE STRONGER RELATIONSHIPS	71
5. CREATE LIFETIME MEMORIES	93
6. WHAT IF...	115
PART 2 - BACK HOME	135
7. FIND GRATITUDE AT HOME	137
8. A VACATION FROM LIFE AS USUAL	141
9. RECHARGE A VACATION HABIT	145
10. BE INTENTIONAL WITH RELATIONSHIPS	149
11. MAKE MEMORIES AT HOME	151
12. DECIDE FOR YOUR FUTURE	153
AFTERWORD	157
QUICK START IDEAS	159
ACKNOWLEDGMENTS	161
AUTHOR	163
READER BONUS	164

GET THE MOST FROM THIS BOOK

To get the most from this book during your vacation:

1. Read one chapter a day.
2. Start with the chapter introduction, a 5-7 minute read.
3. Browse through the 30-60 activities themed to that day.
4. Pick 1-2 activities to do, then have fun!
5. Repeat a chapter if you have more than six days of vacation.
6. Back home, ease into things with the suggestions in Part 2.
7. Check out the QUICK START IDEAS in the back of the book, which include 50+ ideas for families as well as ideas for couples.

P.S. To help you start your vacation STRESS-FREE, I created the ultimate guide to prepare for any trip, and it's free! To download your free planner, go to:

bestvacationeverbook.com

INTRODUCTION

You Deserve a Real Vacation

Pop quiz time! Are you ready? Here we go—

Wait, hold up!! What did you say? There's a quiz? In the first sentence? Why would you open a book with a quiz? Especially a book about vacations! Not to mention, there's been literally nothing written yet. How can you test us on...nothing!?

Okay, settle down. Yes, I admit issuing a quiz is an unconventional way to open a book. Also, you're right, who gives a quiz in a book about vacations? But wait, I do have a point and I'll get to it quickly. After all, we're on vacation. We're here for fun!

P.S., don't worry, it's not the kind of book with lots of quizzes. In fact, this may be the only quiz in the entire book (NOTE TO SELF: see if I have any other quizzes; if so, delete them.)

Back to the quiz. Here it is: think about a recent vacation you've taken. Got one in mind? Great! Now, on the third night of the trip, when you were having dinner, IF you enjoyed some kind of alcoholic beverage, what did you have? Name the drink. That's the quiz.

That's my question: what kind of beverage did you drink on the third night of vacation?

Now, you might say, Thor — by the way, nice to meet you Dear Reader, I'm Thor. You say, I know exactly what I had to drink on the third night of my vacation two years ago. To which I'd say, *really, do tell.*

You might say, I had my usual, a glass of Kendall-Jackson Chardonnay. To which I would say, no way! You can't possibly remember that! Or maybe you can. If so, well done, congratulations on your remarkable memory and/or consistency.

Between friends though, I'm guessing you don't remember exactly what you had. First, let's define remember.

You might "remember" what kind of drink it was. But do you remember the *experience*? The way the glass felt in your hand, the way the candlelight refracted in the glass, the colors of the liquid, the conversation that accompanied each sip. Do you remember *that*?

If you're like most of us, you don't. Consuming that drink was just part of your vacation. It wasn't special, it wasn't unique. Honestly, if you were having a drink, you were just "relaxing." You were on vacation.

WE REMEMBER EXPERIENCES, NOT DETAILS

I know this from first-hand experience. I was in Hawaii last year on vacation. If I took the quiz myself, I wouldn't even remember where we ate on the third night of vacation. It *might* have been Duke's Waikiki. Good place. Nice atmosphere. In fact, that's what I remember most: where we sat. And here's why I remember that.

This vacation was during COVID. In between variants, we were fortunate to be able to travel. But restaurants in Hawaii had struggled during the pandemic. Many closed. Reservations were hard to come by. Like, "You should've made your reservation two months ago."

When I called Duke's, they said they were booked for the entire week. All they could offer was bar seating. Meaning, I assumed, we'd be sitting at a table in the bar area. Duke's is an open-air restaurant, right on Waikiki Beach. I thought "bar seating" would be okay. I said yes.

On the night of our reservation, we arrived at 6 p.m., expecting to be seated at a bar booth, or even at the bar counter. Instead, the hostess led us outside toward the beach-side patio. While following her, I thought, "Are we sitting outside?" My hopes began to rise.

Arriving at our table, I could hardly believe our luck. We had the best seat in the house. Tiki torches lit the patio. Palm trees swayed in literal tropical breezes. A live band played Hawaiian classics. And we had a view of Diamond Head in the night sky.

This was a perfect evening. That's what I remember. The *experience* of dining in that unique location. The karma of it happening in a completely unexpected way.

If you asked me what I drank that night, I'd have no clue. I would fail my own quiz. But I will always remember that evening.

In case you think I remember last year's vacation because it's fresh in my memory, I say *au contraire*. I can go back through 20 years of trips to Hawaii (not every year, mind you). I don't remember whether I had a piña colada or a mai tai by the pool.

But I do remember a hike to the top of Diamond Head. I remember the drive to the North Shore of Oahu, a visit to the beach where the TV show *Lost* was filmed and later, a stop at Matsumoto Shave Ice.

Science confirms why we recall some things and not others. Researchers have found we're substantially more likely to remember experiences that include emotion, and the more vivid the emotion, the stronger the memory.

In my case, I remember our evening at Duke's because the surprise (emotion) of our table location was so strong. I remember going to Matsumoto because of the fear (emotion) of seeing bees swarm a trashcan packed with empty containers of flavor syrup.

Bottom line, we're more likely to recall experiences with vivid emotions. Whereas details such as what we drink, what we eat, or the shave ice flavor — not so much.

The takeaway from this is when we go on vacation, we should look to fill our time with emotional experiences, as opposed to indulgences.

EXPERIENCE VS. INDULGENCE

What's an indulgence? And why is a modern vacation more likely to depend on indulgence than experience? Good question.

We used to think of indulgence as something rich, decadent, frivolous and definitely rare. Eating dinner at a restaurant with a neon sign advertising "Steak and Cocktails." Staying in a Holiday Inn instead of "imposing" on relatives. Ordering any dessert that involved flames, like Baked Alaska or Cherries Flambe.

These days, an "indulgence" is a lot simpler. For example, sleep. As in, more of it, please. Waking up without an alarm. Taking an hour away from texts and emails. Going to the mall for no actual reason.

An indulgence today would be something we should allow ourselves, but don't. See if any of these "indulgences" (and our excuses) hit home:

- Reading a book for an hour during the afternoon. (*Are you kidding? I've got laundry to do, a garage to clean.*)
- Attending a yoga class. (*Love to, but I have to make cupcakes for the soccer team party.*)
- Taking a nap without setting my alarm for exactly 24 minutes. (*Heresy! I need to maximize my sleep today.*)

Since we don't have time for indulgences like these in our normal "working life," we save them all up for the one time of year that belongs to us. Our vacation!

Yes, on vacation, you can do ALL the things you don't normally do at home. You can sleep! You can eat! You can drink! And for many of us, we do all those things in mass quantities.

You begin to mythologize the vacation as the perfect antidote to everything stressful in life. There's no problem that can't be solved by a great one-week vacation, right? Because you can do, be and have it ALL for this one week a year.

It's perhaps not a coincidence the all-inclusive vacation has become so popular with modern travelers.

The concept was pioneered by Club Med after World War II. The idea was to provide French families a vacation filled with fun, sports, games, and entertainment. Mass consumption wasn't the point. Rather, you went to have a meaningful experience.

Things started to change in the 1990s, when companies like Sandals, as well as the burgeoning cruise industry, began to provide a vacation experience more closely associated with a Roman bacchanal.

You could eat as much as you want, whenever you want. You could swim *and* consume alcohol at the same time, thanks to the swim-up bar. Games, activities, entertainment, even waterparks — it was all brought directly to you. Your vacation was right at your feet. Feet that you barely had to move to enjoy your week of indulgence.

To be fair, there's nothing wrong with a little indulging. After all, you work hard 51 weeks a year. Is it too much to ask for one week to enjoy yourself, to do whatever you want? No, not at all.

But let me ask you a question. Are you getting the full value of that week off? How are you spending your time?

Yes, you have seven days off. But how many of those days are you really, truly "off?" The answer may surprise you.

THE TWO-DAY VACATION?

Let's examine the supposed week-long vacation. Instead of starting on day one, let's first consider the week before your vacation. Maybe your to-do list includes the following:

- Print out documents and verify you have everything you need.
- If there's flying involved, you have to confirm flights and seats.
- If you have an office job, you'll need to wrap up big projects.
- You'll need to send "I'm going on vacation" emails.
- You have to plan who's watching your house and pets.
- You need to review your clothing needs.
- You may have to shop for sundries.

...STRESSED YET? WAIT, THERE'S MORE!

- Assuming you have all your clothing, it's time to pack.
- How much can you fit and not exceed the airline baggage limit?
- What food or snacks will you bring for the trip?
- If you have young kids, how will you entertain them?
- When should you leave? Will there be traffic?

The point of all of this is that getting ready to go can make you feel like you need a vacation from your vacation.

(P.S., to alleviate some of this stress, I created the ultimate planning guide to help prepare for any trip, and it's free. Yes, FREE! For an antidote to those stressful weeks before travel, go to...

bestvacationeverbook.com

...and download my FREE *Countdown to Vacation* guide. It's a day-by-day checklist of exactly what do, so you can start your trip in the most blissful state possible. Did I mention it's **free**? Go get it!)

So yes, the week before your travel can feel so overwhelming that you spend the first 2–3 days of your vacation just recovering.

You sleep, you drink, and you avoid doing anything too strenuous. This is the indulgence part of your trip. You learn the location of all the swim-up bars. You became best friends with the spa receptionist. The pool waitress knows you by first name. And of course, dessert isn't a splurge, it's a necessity! After all, you need some serious downtime from all the work it took just to get here.

When you think about it, the first third of your vacation is spent recovering from preparing for your vacation. But that's okay because out of your seven days of vacation, you still have four days left, right? *Right?* Well, let's look at that next.

We'll skip through the middle of your vacation and preview the ending. Yes, the last two days of your trip are likely to be spent preparing to head home: checking flights, reviewing your resort or cruise bill. Looking at your schedule for the week you return, calendaring things to do, laundry, food shopping, childcare.

You may also already be checking out *mentally*. With just days left, you're now realizing the things you won't have time to do on vacation. The restaurants you won't visit. The excursions and sites you won't see. The rides you won't go on. The ambitions ("learn to surf") that will go unrealized.

A kind of sadness can fall over the last few days. Sadness, as you mourn for what could have been and what you wish for. This mythical vacation week, that was going to solve all your life's woes, turns out to be mortal after all. It's like discovering Superman doesn't care about you at all. So let's review...

During the first third of your vacation, you're recovering; you're not fully present.

In the last third you're already checking out; again, you're not present.

So for many of us, it's that middle third of the vacation, roughly 2–3 days, where we get to enjoy ourselves. We're recovered, we're relaxed, we're fun, we're playful, and we're having a good time. But that's only a handful of days, at best.

When you add it all up, in a weeklong vacation, you get to enjoy two whole days. I'll say that again, this time in bold: **in one week off, you probably enjoy 2–3 days.**

Some vacation, right? There must be a better way, you say.

If you're going to take a weeklong vacation, shouldn't the trip itself feel like an entire seven days?

You paid for it. You should get the value of it. *The question is, how?*

THE BOOK THAT CHANGED MY LIFE

My journey on this path started years ago on a trip to Hawaii. Sitting by the pool every day at the Waikiki Beach Marriott, I read a non-fiction book that would have a profound impact on my life. The book itself isn't important. Today, there are 20 other books I'd recommend instead. (DM me @thorchallgren if you really must know the book.) But for me, at that exact time, it was perfect. It wasn't the book itself, but the combination of reading stimulating ideas in an idyllic setting.

I would sit by the pool reading during the day. Inspiring thoughts would combine with the scenery. I'd glance from a sentence to a view of the ocean. Flipping pages in the warm sun, contemplating thoughts while staring at palm trees. It was all just ONE experience. Thought, setting, inspiration.

I came away from the experience uplifted, positive, and excited for the opportunities awaiting me back home.

As an avid traveler myself, I began to see a pattern in the mindset of the people I met on vacation: everyone wants an experience that renews and recharges them. But they also yearn for something deeper.

That's why you are now holding this book. I believe if you approach your vacation more intentionally, you are more likely to create memorable experiences.

By being present in your travel, and by fully inhabiting the moments, you will get to experience the entire vacation. How do you do this?

In *Best Vacation Ever*, I share 300-plus ways to enhance your travel experience. I call them "Awareness Openers," "Awesome Opportunities" or A.O.'s for short.

Themed around areas like renewal, relationships, personal growth, creativity, and focus, the book will give you easily adopted activities, games, and suggestions on how to transform each vacation day into an experience worth savoring. You won't just be indulging yourself; you'll be enriching yourself.

As a lifelong student of fulfillment, I've consumed hundreds of books and courses on how to bring meaning to our lives. I share those decades of wisdom in this book.

You may have read a book like this before. Maybe at year-end, when you were setting resolutions. Why not bring that New Year's experience to your vacation?

In your hands, you have a unique book about something exciting (your life!); something romantic (why not love your vacation?); and something thoughtful (how to make this your best vacation ever.)

SO HOW DOES THIS WORK?

First off, let's not use the "W" word around here, okay? We're here for fun, not work! We're here for the experience. Because remember, experiences are what you remember.

Here's how I recommend you experience the book. The first six chapters can be read over six days of vacation. Of course, you may be on vacation for longer than six days — more on that in a second.

While on vacation, I recommend you read one chapter a day.

The opening of each chapter will be 5-10 minutes of reading (this introduction is a little longer.) After a quick introduction, you'll find

30–60 Awareness Openers themed to the topic that day. Pick two A.O.'s and have fun.

There are 300-plus A.O.'s in the book, so there's plenty of potential for fun. There are games, activities, and ideas to enrich your travel experience. Most are simple and can easily be incorporated into your day, no matter how hectic.

By doing them, you'll see your vacation in a whole new light. Instead of just indulging, you'll become immersed in the experience.

The fun you have will be more profound, you'll discover new insights about yourself, you'll make more meaningful memories, and you'll return home (eventually) with a greater sense of who you are and how to keep the fun going.

I've made starting super easy. In the back of the book, I've included Quick Start Ideas, where I lay out 2–3 A.O.'s per day that progressively build the entire week. I've also highlighted 50-plus activities that are perfect for kids and suggestions for couples as well. You can use either of those, or you can just flip through the section at random and pick A.O.'s that appeal to you.

I can confidently say if you read one section per day — a 10-minute commitment — and you thoughtfully apply just one or two ideas, you will return home more refreshed, energized, and with a new outlook on life that will improve your post-vacation experience.

You don't even have to read the book cover to cover. You can pick whichever section you feel inspired to read, start there, and see which vacay tips appeal to you most. It's really that easy.

If your vacation experience is seven days or longer (lucky you!), I recommend repeating a chapter that appeals to you. Or maybe you saw A.O.'s you didn't get to. Do those!

Think of this book like Orlando. Not the city, but the collection of mega theme parks. Unless you've got a month of vacation time, you (probably) can't go on every single ride at every resort. But you can pick your favorites, and enjoy the experience of being on the ride. Which is what I hope you'll do here.

BUT WHAT IF I WANT TO JUST A "BEACH READ"?

Did you ever wonder why airports have so many bookshops? Maybe it's because people like us are picking up the latest bestseller or paperback classic for the trip ahead.

We have time on the plane, and then time at the beach, or the cafe, or on the ship. We want something to occupy our time.

At that "New Release" table, you might find a mystery thriller, with ordinary people risking it all against a cynically corrupt system.

Or a romance read, featuring modern heroines sorting through life and love. You'd see a spy adventure with undercover double agents risking it all. Or perhaps an inspiring biography of a self-made business titan, or that "My Quirky Life" book written by a popular comedian.

Any of these books could serve as a perfectly acceptable beach, airplane, cafe, or vacation read. Whether they are fiction or non-fiction, most of these books have one fundamental thing in common, one reason why we choose to pick up, read, and hopefully finish that book.

They are stories about people experiencing something unique.

We read these books because we want to experience a different life.

One that's not our life.

Maybe reading and vacations are inextricably linked because both are forms of escapism.

So sure, you could go on vacation without a book like this. Hey, I get it. I understand your vacation time is precious. You want a little R&R, and for many of us, reading means escapist fiction. Raise your hand if that describes you. I'm raising my hand by the way.

But WHAT IF you could bring one escapist book AND bring this book?

You could look back on this vacation, years from now, and remember this as the first time you began to see a bigger, fuller, more alive way to live your life. And it all started on vacation.

HOW DID YOU FIND THIS BOOK?

You could've found this book in any number of ways. You saw it online. A friend recommended it. I gave you a copy.

However it happened, you found this book, and it found you. That's not a small thing. Of all the potential things that could've happened in your life, this one thing DID happen. A book found its way to you.

You're now on a path to new ideas and ways of looking at life. You're participating in an experiment of sorts, where you're evaluating those concepts and applying them to your life to achieve the desired result. That's the first reason you're reading the book.

But you're also reading it because something about the idea appealed to you. I have a hunch you know there is something bigger out there waiting for you and maybe, just maybe, it's going to START on this vacation. Wouldn't that be an experience to remember?

Just like me reading that book years ago, this could be the experience you look back on. The ideas you're about to read have been proven to create happier, more fulfilling lives.

People have been following advice like this for over 100 years. They have seen their lives, careers, health, and relationships improve immensely. Imagine what this kind of positive thinking will do for you when you read and implement it on vacation.

Your week is about to get a whole lot better. Let's go on vacation!

1

MAKE GRATITUDE YOUR SUPERPOWER

55 Ways to Feel More Awesome

Welcome to your vacation! You may be reading this as you travel to your destination, or perhaps you're already there. In either case, we'll have the same focus today: gratitude and appreciation.

You've probably read about the importance of expressing gratitude in life. Often the concept is framed as a means to get something you want. As in, the more grateful you are, the more good things will come to you. This can be true.

But I want to focus on a simpler, more profound reason for adopting this practice. Expressing gratitude for the blessings in your life simply feels good. And since you're on vacation, feeling good is an okay concept to get behind, right?

When you're traveling, there are so many things for which you can express gratitude. For our purposes, let's consider two in particular: things and people. By things, I'm referring to all the extraordinary external things which make your experience possible, such as airplanes, cars, hotels, ships, etc. By people, I'm referring to the vast group of human beings who serve you and improve your experience.

Start by looking around. If you're reading this chapter on an airplane, consider for a moment how utterly amazing that is. *You are flying! On an airplane.* (If you're not flying right now, imagine you are. Remember, you're on vacation!)

Let's pause for a moment and appreciate everything contributing to this experience. If you are flying to Hawaii, for example, marvel at what makes that possible:

- An airline exists to take you exactly where you want to go. *Thank you!*
- People work at an airline whose job is to take you to Hawaii. *Mahalo!*
- A ticket agent checked your bag so you don't have to carry it. *Merci!*
- The TSA people made sure you were safe. *Grazie!*
- The restaurants in the terminal fed you. *Awesome, appreciate it!*
- The gate personnel boarded you smoothly—

"Hold on there," you might be saying. Your plane did *not*, in fact, board in an orderly process. Maybe you were rushed, pushed, and harried. However, we're going to put that all aside right now.

We're going to take a vacation from looking at what's wrong. Today we're going to focus on what's going well. When your vacation's over, you can start looking at what's wrong again. I promise. Wrong is always there. For now, we're looking at the things going right.

Okay, you're back on the plane, hopefully, a little more relaxed...

So yes, you're flying at 35,000 feet, where there's no air, yet you're breathing just fine. Your plane has food, drinks, and a bathroom. You are literally 6–7 miles in the air, and you can go to the bathroom. That doesn't happen every day, does it?

Look out the window. Nothing to see but the ocean. Hours and hours of flying over the ocean. Now think about the pilots. They've trained and logged thousands of hours, so they know exactly how to get your plane to a little island in the vast Pacific ocean.

Sophisticated instruments steer them to precisely the right location. Every time they take off for Hawaii, they manage to find it. No trial and error. They nail the landing! And you don't have to do a thing except sit back and enjoy the ride. *Pretty amazing, huh?*

Another way to look at this is to compare your situation to the past. Before the advent of jet travel in the 1960s, a flight to Hawaii would've taken you— *wait, hold up, you didn't even have a realistic flight option to Hawaii.* You would've taken an ocean liner.

And that trip would've taken 5–7 days, which means that just to visit Hawaii, you would've needed 2–3 weeks of vacation time. So, when you think about it, it's not very likely the average person would have even been able to visit Hawaii. But if you had, it would've been way more expensive than what you'd pay today. So be grateful for that.

Think about your destination as well. Let's say you've flown to a beach resort somewhere in the world. You are more than likely staying in a hotel. If so, be grateful for your accommodations.

Really, be grateful for a hotel?

Well, yes. Think about it. You might be sitting on the most amazing beach in the world. But at the end of the day, if you have no hotel room to sleep in, no restaurant to dine in, no bar in which to enjoy a frozen tourist cocktail — well, I think you can see that being at the most amazing beach in the world won't be much use if you don't have a hotel to stay in.

You'd be no better off than Tom Hanks in *Castaway*. You'd have a beach, Wilson the Volleyball and you'd lose 100 pounds from starvation.

And yet, not only do you have a hotel to return to, but it has been stocked for your complete enjoyment. There are restaurants, bars, and amenities created for your pleasure. So yes, be grateful for your accommodations!

Speaking of eating and drinking, let's also give some thought to that. Perhaps you are reading this at a cafe in Paris, or a diner near a national park. A vast network of people has worked behind the scenes to stock that cafe or diner with exactly what's required to service your order.

Just for a moment, stare at that cup of coffee and think of all the people who worked to bring it to you. The coffee may have only cost $4.50 but think of all the things you didn't have to do.

You didn't have to grow the beans. You didn't have to ship the beans from their tropical home to the facility where they would be roasted and packaged. You didn't have to ship them to the cafe. You didn't have to get up at 4 a.m. to brew the coffee. You just had to step up to the counter, place your order, and get your name spelled wrong.

Or perhaps you didn't even have to do that. Maybe you just sat at your table, and someone came by to ask what you'd like. And then moments later, they brought it to you! Isn't that worth a few dollars? I know for me, not having to grow my own Arabica beans on a tropical farm is easily worth a couple of bucks.

Do you know what else you don't have to do on vacation? Make your bed! That's right. When you're at home, you must make your bed, hang up your towels, and tidy up your bedroom space.

But when you are on vacation, there is someone paid to do that. They come in every day and make your bed, give you fresh towels, mop the bathroom floor, vacuum the carpet, clean the sink, and restock your coffee and tea supplies. Often, they'll even tidy up, arranging your toothbrush on the sink and organizing your clothes.

Do you have that kind of service at home? I don't. So when I go on vacation, I'm grateful for these amenities, because I know that when I get home, I'm the one who has to make my coffee, meals, and bed.

Now a quick note. All these people are here to make your vacation better. Do they always succeed? No, of course not.

You may on occasion receive poor or indifferent service. They may forget to bring you something. Your plane may be late. A bag may be lost. You may have to wait longer than you'd like for the airport transfer. Your room may not immediately be ready. Things may not be perfect.

But remember, even in those moments when things don't happen exactly the way we want, those people are still working, putting out the effort to make your experience better.

"Yes, but you don't understand," I hear you saying. "My flight was HORRIBLE. The plane was late, the seats were cramped, the flight attendant was rude, and—"

Stop!

Everyone's doing the best they can. Remember, they're the ones working. You are the one on vacation. Things may not be perfect and you may face challenges. You paid good money for your trip, and you have a right to expect decent service and good value.

But when you're focused on how crappy things are, you are NOT in a vacation state of mind. Every second you spend in an upset and angry state of mind, well, you're not on vacation. And you didn't take a week off to be in this mood, did you? No!

So make a decision, right now. Act on what you can change at the moment. Politely but firmly ask for what you want. Insist things be made right. Then move on to a better feeling thought. Appreciate what you have and where you are.

The key to all this is to open your eyes and awareness to things that, up until now, you may have taken for granted. Often, we're so busy with our lives, getting things done, doing what's necessary, that we're not aware of everything that happens without us knowing it. We don't take the time to appreciate what we have. So let's start today.

Here are several Awesome Openers — A.O.'s — you could choose to do today. They are games, reflections, and suggestions on how to bring gratitude into your day. Glance through the list and choose 1–2 ideas that resonate with you. Then focus on doing those today.

If you keep a vacation journal, which I highly recommend, write down the A.O.'s you like. Once you complete them, make a few notes about what they meant to you.

If you see more than a few ideas that you vibe with, circle them. At the end of the week, we'll have a plan for what to do with them.

P.S. If you're reading this before you travel, check out my free printable Vacation Journal PDF at www.bestvacationeverbook.com.

Okay, let's get started!

START WITH GRATITUDE

1. THREE THINGS. Starting right now, find three things you can be grateful for. Yes, right this moment. Quick! Don't overthink it. Just look around. Find three things that make you happy. Write those down.

Maybe it's that pretty palm tree. Or the service you're receiving. The taste of that drink. The color of the pool water. The stillness of the sunrise. It doesn't have to be big, or momentous. You can be grateful for big things or small things. In fact, if you're grateful for lots of small things, that creates more consistent positive energy than infrequent gratitude for big things. Okay, write them down.

A NOTE FROM THOR... Okay, that was one thing you did. Do you see how easy that was? You just looked around, and you noticed one thing, then another, and a third. You wrote them down. Easy, right? Easy is what we're going for.

2. START WITH YOURSELF. If you found #1 difficult, or it seemed silly or frivolous to list three things you're grateful for, make it easy on yourself. Just be grateful for yourself. You. Specifically, consider what you will be able to do on this vacation.

Here's what I mean. If you can walk, if you can get around, be grateful. If you can swim, hike or jog, be grateful. If you can surf— "Wait, hold on," you're thinking. "I'm not here to surf." Well, maybe not. But imagine if you were, and you had a twisted ankle, which would prevent you from surfing. But it's not twisted, so you could go surfing if you wanted. Be grateful for that, and all the other things you can do on this vacation! Again, just like with #1, write down three things about your situation, for which you can be grateful. Begin each sentence, "I can...", or "I get to..."

THOR AGAIN, HERE... Have you seen how this works? If you did both of those, you've now brought some gratitude into your vacation. If you're like, "Hey, that was easy. I wonder if there are more ideas I can implement?" Why yes, there are. I invite you to keep reading. It's always okay to do more than 1 or 2 things in a day.

3. THOSE AROUND YOU. Once you've focused on what you appreciate about yourself, expand your focus to those around you.

Your spouse, kids, parents, friends — whoever is traveling with you, think to yourself what you appreciate about them. Be specific.

For example, you might say, "I'm grateful to my husband for taking the kids sailing so that I can enjoy some 'me time.'" Or "I'm grateful for my friend who is willing to share this trip with me."

HEY THERE, POTENTIAL OVERACHIEVER, THOR AGAIN... If you identify with the "overachiever" label, you might be thinking right now, "This is going great. I'm going to do ALL of these!" I love this unbridled enthusiasm, I really do. But I will say, "Whoa there, 'Tex."

Don't feel you have to put a red checkmark next to each exercise you've completed. It's not a race. Do what feels right. Be led to enjoy the experience. I don't want your vacation to become some personal development death march. I can't have you keeling over. That would be very bad for you, and the book sales. Okay, back to the list...

4. BEFORE YOU RISE. If you like these exercises, try practicing gratitude before you get out of bed tomorrow. Before your feet hit the floor, find three things you are grateful for on this trip. They can be simple or big, your choice. But start your day with gratitude.

Next, do something that author Pam Grout recommends in her book, *Thank and Grow Rich*. After saying your three things, say, "Something amazing and wonderful is coming my way today." I love that! By doing this, you're training your mind to watch for amazing things. And guess what? If you're looking, you'll likely find 'em.

5. MAKE A LIST. While in a setting you might normally take for granted, make a list of things you appreciate. Emphasize things you don't normally focus gratitude on. If you're at a restaurant table, your list might include salt and pepper, ketchup, hot sauce, sugar, clean silverware, napkins, or ice water. Often, we take these for granted, but imagine your life without them. If you've ever traveled to a place that doesn't have ketchup, you know how much you appreciate having it. So really, #5 could be labeled, "Appreciate Ketchup."

THOR HERE AGAIN... Before we get to #6, I'm now going to give you an idea you could use if you are traveling with kids. There are over 50 kid-friendly ideas throughout the book. If you want a list, flip to the back. If you AREN'T traveling with kids, consider that as a bonus thing to be grateful for (I'm kidding, of course.) (Yeah, sort of not.)

6. TAG, YOU'RE GRATEFUL! If you're traveling with kids, ask them something they love about this destination. Follow up with why they love it. You could even make it a "you're it!" game. Start the game by saying, "I love .... because .... " then tag them or say "you're it!"

If you've started a vacation journal (or if you downloaded the free PDF journal page I have at bestvacationeverbook.com) write down what they share. Trust me, years from now, you will treasure memories of what stood out to them at this age.

7. HOW LUCKY ARE WE? Remind yourself how lucky you are to be in this location. You might say out loud, "I am so lucky to be here right now." Yup, nothing wrong with a little affirmation. Think about it. There are untold thousands (or millions) of people who'd love to be in your place right now. If you're in Italy, for example, realize there are vast numbers of people whose dream in life is to visit Italy someday. There may also be people who had that dream and yet never made it. So for you, getting to be there right now? That's a pretty good deal. Why not affirm this by saying, "I'M LUCKY TO BE HERE!"

8. EVERYTHING IS POSSIBLE. Take five minutes and list all the things you can do on this vacation. Without stopping, write down as many things as you can think of. Then look at the list and realize how much there is to do. If you are on a cruise, your list might include: sit by the pool, go rock climbing, see an evening show, catch a comedy act, do a wine tasting, get a massage, order room service, take a spinning class, read in the library, go sailing, get your hair or nails done, enter the sexiest legs contest (men), judge the sexiest legs contest (ladies), take a dancing class, play bingo, go shopping, write postcards [takes a breath] well, you get the idea. Seeing your list on paper can be surprising. Yes, you have a lot of options. Be grateful for that.

9. OH, WHAT A FANTASTIC DAY! At dinner, take out your vacation journal, or whatever notebook you're writing in, and jot down 2–3 of your favorite experiences today. If you're traveling with others, share with them. Ask what they loved the most. Another "share" could be, what was your happiest moment? Decide to go back at the end of the week and look at all your responses. Maybe you could re-copy all of these onto a page called, "Look at All The Fun Things I Did."

KID'S VARIATION OF #9: Give a prize to the "winner" who has the most creative "favorite," or who expressed the most gratitude.

10. SINGLE-MINDED FOCUS. Find one thing in your day and focus exclusively on that. Maybe it's an object, a place, or a situation. Think about that thing, its purpose, its history, its benefit to others, and let yourself feel appreciation for it.

Maybe you're in Paris, and you're thinking of the Eiffel Tower. Feel gratitude for all the visitors it entertains, for the views it affords, for the millions who have fallen in love with it, for the way it looks at sunset, or at night. Just don't take a picture of it at night; I hear you can't do that for some legal reason.

11. POSTCARDS! Write three postcards in which you describe to the recipients what you love about visiting this place. Emphasize your description and share in the note what it means to you. You might begin the postcard with words like, "I love this .... because" and then list three things you love about it.

KID'S VARIATION OF #11: If your kids don't yet write, offer to write their notes for them. Ask what they like and write down exactly what they say. You could send these kinds of postcards to yourself as a vacation keepsake.

12. I CAN CALL THE OFFICE IF I WANT! Okay, bear with me here. I don't want to talk about work, but this is important. If you have a job that requires you to be in contact, even while on vacation, realize how lucky you are. Yes, I know. Most people wouldn't consider it a good thing to have to stay in touch with the office or their business.

But when you realize that cell coverage reaches around the globe, maybe you could think about this with *some* level of appreciation. After all, you can be thousands of miles away from work, perhaps drinking a piña colada on the beach (this seems to be my go-to drink in this book, doesn't it?), and despite drinking on the beach, you can still put out work fires if need be. Do you know what the potential alternative is to not having wi-fi? No vacation. Be grateful for that.

13. FACETIME THE KIDS! If you have kids, and you are traveling without them, let's say a great big thanks to FaceTime, Zoom, or whatever instant access video service that allows you to check-in

back home. You might not have taken a trip away from the kids 20 years ago when international phone calls were super expensive.

But now you can relax in your fancy beach chair in the Caymans, sipping a piña colada (OMG, there it is again! What's going on with me and piña coladas??), and you're looking at the dreamy blue ocean, and telling your kids on FaceTime that "Mommy misses you a lot." And you might even mean it.

14. REPEAT AFTER ME: THIS IS VACATION. Part of your "job" is to relax. Too often, we jam our days full of activities. We don't want to miss anything. As a result, we come home and inevitably say, repeat after me, "I need a vacation from my vacation." Try not to be that person. Have reasonable expectations of what you can do on vacation. Build-in free time to do nothing if you want. If I know there's a day filled with activity, I'll schedule open time the next day. Be grateful you have this time to relax.

15. DO A GRATITUDE DANCE. You have a gratitude dance, right? The kind of dance you do at home when things go amazingly well. If you don't have one, guess what? You're going to make one up! Find a piece of music you like grooving to, for example, maybe the piña colada song (That's it! That's why I'm so fixated on that drink. Whew, I'm glad we solve that mystery.) Pick a song that, when it plays, you can't sit still. Now play that music. And dance. With abandon. With joy. With gratitude. There, now you have a gratitude dance. If you're traveling with a friend, spouse, or family, you could do a collective dance of vacation appreciation.

REALIZE HOW MUCH ALREADY GOES RIGHT

16. WHAT YOU DIDN'T HAVE TO DO. List three things you didn't have to do today and feel appreciation for that. For most of us, this is easy. We didn't have to shop for food, make meals, do the dishes, etc. Maybe you just looked at a menu and said "I'll have that." Take a moment to appreciate this. You probably also didn't have to make your bed, clean the bathroom, vacuum, etc. You also didn't have to work. These are all things for which to be grateful.

17. AT LEAST I'M NOT IN SCHOOL. Here's a fun kid's idea. Have them write down three things they didn't have to do today. Answers might include, "homework," "take out the trash," or "make my bed."

Remind them how much fun vacation is. If you have kids who aren't huge fans of school, and you find them complaining about something on vacation, you could remind them, "Hey, at least you aren't in math class" (or P.E., or English, or whatever subject they don't like.) If they're teens, and you remind them of this, they will most likely look at you like you're a weird alien. That's okay. You're an alien on vacation!

18. THREE TIMES. So often, things go smoothly, and we don't stop to notice. Our suitcases *usually* make it off the plane, our hotel room is *often* ready on time. Our meals are served to us in a timely fashion. Usually, we take that for granted. But not today. Be aware of three people who served you today and notice when things went well. Maybe it's the person who brought your breakfast, the ride-share driver who arrived right on time, or the housekeeper who cleaned your room while you were away. Whoever it is, jot down in your vacation journal (or notes) the three times things went well.

19. HOW DID THEY KNOW? When something goes right, as it usually does, say out loud, in a delighted fashion, "How Did They Know?" Then spend a minute marveling at how everything aligned just right at that moment. Let's say it's a bartender who remembers your favorite drink after just one day at the resort. This has happened to me at the Beaches in Negril, Jamaica. The friendly bartender offered me a "hummingbird" cocktail on my first day. From then on, he remembered me and the fact that I liked the drink. I spent time wondering how he could remember me with all the guests he had to serve. And yet he did!

20. WHEN THINGS GO RIGHT. Make a "What Went Right" playlist. Imagine the events of your life are an album playlist with song titles. Now title each thing that went right today as if it were the name of a track on the album. Create your playlist of things that went perfectly well today.

BE NICE TO PEOPLE

21. WHAT I LIKE ABOUT YOU! You're having a lovely vacation dinner with your travel companion (or family.) Everyone's in a great mood. Find a moment sometime during the meal to have everyone share one thing they appreciate about each other. Find something specific. If you have a large group, maybe limit each person's time to 2–3 shares.

You go last, to make sure if someone was missed, you can use your time to share about them.

KIDS VARIATION OF #21: If you have young ones at the table, challenge them to be specific in their moment of appreciation. Saying "I appreciate that Daddy took me fishing today" is more specific than "I like Daddy because he's nice."

22. A HALLMARK MOMENT. Here's one for couples! Write a thank-you note to your travel partner or spouse. Tell them something you appreciate about them. Thank them for small things, or big things.

For example, you might say, "I appreciate that you lifted my heavy suitcase into the overhead bin on the plane" (small thing) or "I love seeing how kind you are to all the people we meet. It's one of the reasons I love you so much (definitely a big thing.) Write out your note (perhaps on hotel stationery if you can find it), locate an envelope, and leave it for your spouse to discover. For bonus points, find some local flowers (pick them, if legal) and arrange them around your note.

23. WHAT GOES AROUND... Let's say you do #22 above for your partner or spouse. And of course, they are going to love you for it. What's next? Turnabout is fair play, right? Show them this page. Point to #22 and say, "Just in case you're interested." By the way, dog-ear the page too. That'll make it easier to find. Essentially, you are encouraging them to reciprocate your kind act. Oh, and while they're at it, suggest they also check out #24 below.

24. DEAR MOMMY OR DADDY. Help your kids write a thank-you note to your spouse. If they were the chief planner for this trip, the note could focus on everything they did to ensure you are having a wonderful time. As above, if the kids are still in the crayon stage, a personal picture showing the happy spouse on the phone or at the computer can be just as meaningful. As a corollary to this, you might also encourage your kids to write a second note, this one to the spouse whose hard work helped pay for this trip. Sometimes that goes unsaid, but truly, there wouldn't even be a vacation if not for the countless hours spent in the office, on the road, or in endless meetings. Remind your kids to be grateful for that as well.

25. THREE PEOPLE. Express your gratitude to three people today. It could be the person who checked you in, the flight attendant

who brought your drink or the room attendant who brought you extra pillows. Whoever it is, thank them for improving your vacation experience. Here's an exact script of what you can say, in case you're a little rusty on this whole gratitude thing: "Thanks very much for .... I really appreciate that."

26. MAKE EYE CONTACT. Pick someone to thank — for example, one of the people in #25. When you express your gratitude, be sure to make eye contact with them. Too often, we drop our "thanks" as we're walking away or we're thinking about the next thing we must do. When your "thanks" is offered more purposefully, it's more likely to be appreciated by them, and will also feel better to you.

27. BE SPECIFIC. Did making eye contact feel good? Great! Now consider adding one more component to your expression of gratitude. When you say thanks, and you make eye contact, also tell the person what you appreciate about their act. You might say, for example, "I'm sure you've been busy this afternoon checking people in, and I really appreciate how easy you've made this experience for me." When you personalize your thanks this way, you're more likely to convey the warmth and genuineness of your appreciation.

28. LEAVE A NOTE. Consider leaving a daily note for your hotel housekeeper. Most of us rarely see the person who picks up after us. We may greet someone from the housekeeping staff in the hallway, but you may not know if they're assigned to your room. Why not write them a quick note and thank them for the service they're providing? If you're in a foreign country where there may be a language barrier, use your smartphone to translate a simple message. If you want to leave a few dollars with the note, that would also be appreciated.

KIDS VARIATION OF #28: Ask your kids to leave a thank you note for the housekeeper. If they're still in the crayon-drawings-are-cute phase, this is a nice way to show their appreciation.

29. THE UNSEEN PEOPLE. Thank someone who normally may not receive compliments. If you see a hotel or resort staff member doing what would be considered a behind-the-scenes job, offer them praise for their role in enhancing the guest experience. Maybe you notice a landscaper trimming the flowers. Compliment them on the beauty of the gardens. If it's someone from the airline helping you check your bag or print out the boarding pass, this would be another excellent

opportunity to say thanks. Especially because this is the kind of worker who rarely hears anything besides, "I'm late for my flight," or "My suitcase can't possibly weigh 55 pounds."

30. WRITE A NOTE. Write a note complimenting someone who went out of their way to help, seal the note, then give it to the front desk and ask them to pass it along to the appropriate manager. Mentioning the person by name and describing how they went above and beyond will be meaningful to that staff member. Hotels and cruise ships often reward and promote employees who receive this kind of praise. If you leave online reviews at sites like TripAdvisor, mention helpful staff members by name. Management often reads these boards and will again take note of standout employees.

31. THANK YOU ARTWORK. Here's another way to engage your kids' talents in expressing their appreciation. Using construction paper and markers, encourage your kids to write a personal note to someone on your trip who has been kind. Whether it's someone in the kids club, a meal server, or someone who may never receive a word of kindness. Imagine how they'll feel receiving a cute note from a smiling child. Now that's kindness!

32. THANK SOMEONE AT HOME. Was there someone at home who helped you plan this trip, or encouraged you to go? Maybe a friend who suggested the destination, or a travel agent who planned your adventure. If so, thank them. This could be a simple text sharing your experience so far, something like "Thanks, friend, for helping me plan this trip. We just (name an activity you did) and we all loved it. I appreciate the suggestions you gave that made this trip special."

33. CALL OR TEXT SOMEONE. RIGHT NOW. Is there someone in your life who has done something nice for you? Give them a call, right now, and tell them how much you appreciate them. To make it easy, pull out your phone and open your texting app. Scroll to the very bottom and find someone you haven't spoken to within a while. Give them a shout, either a call or text. Sometimes the text might be easier.

What would you say after all this time has passed? Podcaster Jordan Harbinger suggests a quick message like this: "Hey ...., Haven't spoken with you in ages. I hope this finds you well. What's up with you? No rush to reply if you're busy, but I'd love to hear what you're up to when you get a chance." If you reach this person, either by phone or text, chances are they'll ask how you are and what you're up to. Should you tell them you're on vacation? That's up to you. If you can do it in a way that doesn't come off as too humble-braggy ("Yeah, just sitting here in a cafe in Katmandu"), go for it. The person you reach might be impressed that, with all the things you could do on vacation, you chose to contact them.

34. RANDOM ACTS OF KINDNESS. In addition to thanking people, consider performing random acts of kindness for others. You could hold a door or offer to lift someone's carry-on bag on the plane. Other ideas: give someone directions to the pool. Give someone tips on your hotel. Buy an espresso for the person in line behind you. Offer your poolside seat to someone who just arrived. Tidy up your dishes while eating out to make your server's job easier.

There are dozens of ways you can find to make other people's lives easier. If you can't think of one, ask yourself, what would I appreciate someone doing for me?

35. HELPFUL KIDS. Encourage your kids to look for ways they can help others. If they're staying in the kids club at the hotel or on a ship, there are likely lots of things they could do for another child or the caregivers at the club. As with #34 above, you might ask them, what do they wish someone would do for them? Then suggest they do that for someone else.

36. HAPPY PLAYLIST. Make a playlist with music that calms you and reminds you to be grateful. If you have a busy day, fire up that playlist, close your eyes (if you're not driving) and enjoy some "your time."

37. AND THE AWARD GOES TO... To encourage your fellow travelers to look for the positive, decide that at the end of your trip, you will have an awards ceremony on your final night. At this event, you'll give out awards for people who best lived up to the ideals of gratitude and appreciation. For example, you could give an award to the person who overcomes a challenge most positively. Hint: find a way to recognize everyone for something they did on the trip, if possible.

This game can work whether you're traveling with one person or a dozen. The only "rule" is that everyone should both give and receive an award. If you have kids, assign their "recipient" at the start of the week and help them choose something to appreciate.

38. MAKE AN APPOINTMENT TO BE NICE. Something else you can do at the end of your trip is to tell each person you're traveling with at least ONE THING you appreciated about them on this trip. Maybe it's something nice they did, or a positive or supportive attitude they brought to a situation. So that you remember to do this, make an appointment in your calendar, whether it's your phone or paper planner. Do it near the end of your trip. "Praise John, 2 p.m., Friday."

39. STRANGERS BEARING GIFTS. Bring gifts to give to people who help you on vacation. You might bring a few boxes of candy, or if your town has a unique cultural item or food, bring that to share. Travel writer JohnnyJet shares how he brings boxes of chocolates to share with the flight crew when he flies. Make sure your gifts are sealed so the recipient receives them with confidence.

You might even pre-print thank you notes to affix to the gift, something like "Thanks for Making Our Trip Special." You could produce these on a computer or create your own decorative stamp.

40. HEY BIG SPENDER! Decide in advance to tip a "large" amount to someone who helps out. You decide what "large" is for you: $20, $50, $100, whatever. The amount doesn't matter. But it should feel a little out of the ordinary for you. Knowing in advance you will do this, be on the lookout for this person. Expect they will appear. Actively consider the service you are receiving, and ask, "Is this the person?"

One of the hidden values of this game is now you'll go through your day (or week) EXPECTING to find a service worthy of this generosity. And when you look for things like this, you tend to find them.

IF (OR WHEN) THINGS DON'T WORK OUT...

41. REMEMBER YOU HAVE A CHOICE. Face it, if you're gone for an entire week, it's possible (nay, probable) that not everything will be 100% perfect. Maybe your flight will be delayed, or the room won't be ready, or you'll face a long wait for your favorite restaurant.

In these moments, remember you have a CHOICE. You always do. You can choose to let this bother you, or you can do what's possible to adjust the circumstances. If that doesn't work, you still have a choice. Adjust your attitude about the problem. Just make a different choice.

42. ON VACATION, IT'S NOT A PROBLEM. Quick grammar point. If you have a "problem" on vacation, and after you affirm that you are, in fact, on vacation, change the way you describe the situation. A "problem" on vacation becomes a "challenge" or an "opportunity." This matters because when something is a "challenge," it means there's a solution. When it's an "opportunity," it means YOU are the person who gets to come up with the solution.

43. CHANGE YOUR RELATIONSHIP TO THE CHALLENGE. You might also change the way you describe your reaction to the situation. Instead of saying, "I'm so angry," or "This pisses me off," find a neutral way to describe your state. You might instead say "I'm very vexed at this moment in time," or "I'm a little bit steamed, bordering on peevishness if you want to know the truth." Yes, have fun with your annoyance, and you'll find your energy about the situation turn from anger to annoyance to tolerance to acceptance, and before you know it, you'll be back on vacation, having a good time.

44. IT'S ACTUALLY YOUR FAULT. Sorry to harsh your groove on vacation, but if something didn't go right, and you're now facing a challenge, it's your fault. I mean, you are there, you are facing the challenge. If you accept responsibility (at least in part), now you can shift to finding a resolution.

If I spend time blaming someone else or arguing over fault, you know what I'm NOT doing? Solving the problem, er... challenge. The sooner you move from blame to acceptance, the sooner you can make things better. And "better" is what you want on vacation, right?

45. OKAY, BUT HOW DO WE SOLVE THE PROB— *UH—* **CHALLENGE?** In trying to resolve the matter, remember: Be patient. Be flexible. Be firm. Be nice. Sometimes when we get unwanted news like "I'm sorry, your room isn't ready," we immediately launch into anger. From that emotion, we're unlikely to find a solution.

Instead, try this: (1) express your understanding of the situation, (2) tell them you do appreciate their efforts on your behalf, (3) explain what your most important need is, and (4) ask for their assistance with something they CAN help with.

For example, you might say, "I understand there doesn't appear to be a room available (1), and I do appreciate everything you're doing to help me (2). We've been flying for 12 hours and the kids would love to change into their suits to go swimming (3). Is there anything you can do to help with that?" (4).

With this approach, you're more likely to enlist their cooperation. And by asking for something simple, you've kept the dialogue going, and they may now be willing to do something for "nice people" like you? Maybe you'll be comped some benefit or amenity that you wouldn't have received by complaining or jumping to an angry tirade. And honestly, this kind of dialogue just feels better.

46. THAT'S OKAY! WE'RE ON VACATION! Here's a specific way to let go of anger or frustration when things go wrong. Every time something doesn't go exactly right, say out loud, "That's okay! We're on vacation!" If you're in an especially desirable place, you might say, "That's okay! We're in Paris!" "That's okay! This is Bora Bora!" I mean seriously, if you're in Paris, and you're having a quote-unquote problem, sorry, but you really don't have a problem. You're in freaking Paris!! Same with Bora Bora.

47. WHAT DON'T I KNOW? Sometimes people do annoying things. Even on vacation. Maybe someone's rude to me, the service is slow, or I don't receive what I expect. When I encounter this kind of situation, I ask myself, "Is there something I don't know?" Maybe there's a reason why things happened as they did, and if you *knew* the reason, it would put your annoyance in context.

What if that server who forgot your order is covering someone else's shift? They're doing double the work. It's not their fault. They're doing the best they can. So always ask yourself, "What else don't I know?" and then respond to unwanted circumstances with a little more understanding.

48. PRAISE BE VACATION! Obliterate complaints with praise. It's inevitable that somewhere along the way, we might find something to complain about. The service was too slow, we received the wrong order, and the ride broke down.

When you find yourself making anything that sounds like a complaint, immediately follow it with a positive observation. This can be a simple statement about anything on your trip, as long as it's positive. Make it a game, and have fun with it.

For example, if you find yourself complaining about waiting for the elevator, you could then quickly add something like, "Well, it might be taking longer than I'd like, but this elevator will take me to the most amazing pool/beach/London street."

KIDS VARIATION ON #48: This is especially good with kids. If they catch Mommy or Daddy complaining, they will delight in reminding you, "Say one positive thing!"

49. RISE ABOVE! Speaking of kids (or even adults sometimes), if you do encounter a complaint-worthy situation, encourage the complainer to treat this situation as an adventure. Did Indiana Jones complain about the boulder? Did Luke Skywalker complain about the Death Star? Did Dora complain about Swiper? No! They treated the situation as an adventure and decided to rise above the challenge. Yes, they could have been miserable (and been crushed or vaporized by a laser blast or outwitted by a fox.) Instead, they decided to rise above the obstacle. Say to all concerned, "Just rise above!"

50. TRADING PLACES. Remind yourself that you could be working here right now instead of relaxing. It could be your job to serve them breakfast, work the hot grill, trim the gardens, haul the luggage up to the rooms, rake the seaweed off the beach, or clean up the messy dishes after lunch. But it's not. It's your "job" to vacation. If you need help, just say to yourself, "I could be doing that." Note that it doesn't mean we denigrate the people doing those jobs, or we think less of them. We can appreciate what they are doing for us, and still be grateful that today, we don't have to do that job.

51. WHAT'S GOING WELL? Above all, resolve to remind yourself how many things go well for you. State that whenever possible. Remind yourself out loud, "Things normally go well for me. I love that!" Or use positive affirmations like, "This is the perfect vacation," "I love this experience," "I'm having such a good time," or "I can handle any challenge that comes my way!"

52. TWO-MINUTE RULE. Okay, tell the truth. You might have read the following ideas and thought, "This positivity stuff is all well and good, but I'm not Gandhi. I'm no saint. If someone annoys me, I want to feel annoyed. I want to be mad." Okay fine, for you, we'll make an exception. If there's a situation that just REALLY peeves you, decide you will complain out loud about it for exactly two minutes. Be as

vocal as you want and let it out. But when you're done, after two minutes, you don't get to talk about it anymore. At all. You're done complaining about that topic. So, if you think you'll feel better by complaining, have at it for two minutes. Then move on.

53. THE OTHER TWO-MINUTE RULE. Give positivity equal time. If you spend two minutes complaining about a situation, balance that out by spending two minutes talking about what you could've done differently, what might be good about your situation, or how you'll be stronger as a result of overcoming this challenge. Yes, you will overcome! Spend equal time talking about that!

54. "LET IT GO!" Finally, if something does go awry, resolve to let it go as soon as possible. Use any of the above tools; whatever you find helpful. Remember, you're the one on vacation, not your problem. Your problem didn't pay for this trip, you did! Don't continue to speak about it, or tell people what went wrong. It happened; you did the best you could to resolve it. Now move on and enjoy the rest of the trip without continually reliving that situation.

55. "NO MATTER WHAT." With the last 14 suggestions, I've tried to convince you to change your P.O.V. about challenges you face. In his book, *Soundtracks*, speaker/author Jon Acuff offers an affirmation to use when you experience problems. Instead of creating an internal dialogue of dissatisfaction, annoyance or anger, replace that negative belief with a new "soundtrack," like "Everything is always working out for me." When you say this, you are re-training your mind to look for the positive opportunity in whatever happened.

One of my mentors, Dr. James Mellon, calls this kind of affirmation an Already Established Premise, or A.E.P. His own personal A.E.P. is, "My life is unfolding perfectly, no matter what." This affirmation is similar to Acuff's, with the addition of "...no matter what." Again, this reminds us that yes, we may face challenges. But no matter what they are, we'll move *through* and past them. And we'll still have an awesome vacation. No matter what.

There's an old story about two monks on a journey. When they come to a river crossing, one of the monks offers to carry an old beggar across the river, despite his friend's annoyance with the beggar.

Once across, the monk puts the beggar down, and he continues with his friend. For the next several miles, the monk who witnessed this act complains about how this slowed them down, and how he would've never offered that assistance. The other monk just listens to these complaints, hour after hour.

Finally, he raises a hand and says, "My friend. I put that beggar down hours ago. Why are you still carrying him?"

The moral of the story is put the complaint down and enjoy the rest of your trip. Good advice for vacations, I'd say.

2

THE POWER OF THE NOW VACATION

55 Ways to Be Present in Paradise

Let me state this again. You're on vacation! Congratulations. Are you feeling it yet? I hope so!

So how was your first day? Are you feeling a new sense of appreciation for where you are, and the experiences you're having? Hopefully you're now approaching your travel with a renewed sense of gratitude. I know I am grateful you've read this far. With that said, let's keep the vacay train rolling!

First, I want to address one possible thought you might be having about the book so far. "Thor," you might say, "I noticed you suggested I implement two of the vacation ideas each day, yet there are 55 ideas in chapter one. Where am I supposed to start exactly?" Okay, that's a fair question. I do acknowledge that some of you may have read every single idea, all 55, then you paused, threw up your hands, and said, "I'm overwhelmed! Where do I start?"

Let me answer your question with a metaphor because I read metaphors make everything simple.

This book is kind of like the experience of visiting a deli for lunch. They give you that giant laminated menu, and you immediately are confronted with 650 choices of things you can order. Okay, maybe that's an exaggeration. Maybe it's only 325. (You see what I did there? 325 items? That's how many are in this book, but you got that.) My point is, there are a lot of things you can eat in a deli. Like pretty much everything. I think you can get tacos and kung pao chicken in a deli, which makes no sense. Anyway, when you're holding that deli menu, you expect you will be able to place an order with your waitress, right? There's no concern you'll have to stand and leave the restaurant in shame, unable to make a choice. NO! You will choose. You will eat. You will pay your bill. It will all work out.

This book is the same way. Yes, there are 325 different ideas. Yes, there were 55 in the last chapter. In case you're the flip-ahead-to-the-end kind of person, there are 55 in this chapter. Honestly, I didn't plan that. I didn't number them until the end. This kind of kismet thing happens when you're on vacation, right?

So yes, there are a lot of things to choose from. But I said it before, and I'll say it again. Don't overwhelm yourself. You're on vacation. Don't be the person who goes on Instagram and Facebook, and boasts about how you did all 325 things in one week, give or take. (Though if you do, please tag me @thorchallgren.) But really, don't do that.

Honestly, I recommend you pick the ones you vibe with, or just seem fun. If you want guidance, remember I have suggested pairings in the back of the book. Kind of like a wine pairing. So you don't have to figure out what pairs well with gratitude. Anyway, check 'em out. If any vibe with you, great. If not, blaze your own path, rebel!

Let's dive into today's theme. Wherever you are, put your feet on the floor or on the ground. You are in this place. Maybe it's a cafe or a train. Or you might be having breakfast at your B&B. Or you're sipping coffee on your balcony, enjoying the sunrise. Wherever you are, one of two things is true. Either you've been to this place before, or it's new to you. That's kind of like Vacationing 101, right? You've been here before, or you haven't.

But let me ask you this: why did you come to this place? Is it because it's new, or because it's familiar? Both possibilities are fine, but let's consider what our choice says about us.

Some people like to travel to new places. There's so much in the world to see, and there's only a certain amount of life to see it all. (Hence the popularity of books like *1001 Places to See Before You Die.*) It's a big world. People want to get out there and experience it, never returning to the same place. Other people like to travel to familiar places. They have their go-to vacations. They may like the amenities or services of a particular hotel or cruise brand.

The type of vacation experience you prefer — new or familiar — could be a reaction to the way your non-vacation life is organized — you know, the other 51 weeks in the year. People who experience lots of newness, uncertainty, or stress in their jobs may be more likely to seek the familiar for their time off. People who have jobs with consistency or sameness may crave more adventure in their travel. And it's possible you might like variety. On one trip, you want uniqueness; on another, you seek familiarity.

Whichever type of vacationer you are, on this trip, why not look at your destination with a new set of eyes? If you've never been to this place, that'll be easy. And even if you have been here, consider seeing it in a new light. In either instance, be curious about the place you're visiting. Be willing to see things in a completely new way. Detach from the familiar. Treat everything as if it was new to you. In Zen Buddhism, this is called "beginner's mind." You clear your mind of all the filters through which you normally process input. Try to view your familiar surroundings with a beginner's vacation mindset.

Here now are some vacation A.O.'s designed to increase your awareness of the new and unique aspects you can find on your vacation. And remember, for heaven's sake, just pick two.

IT'S ALL-NEW

56. READING IS FUNDAMENTAL. Whether or not you've previously been to this destination, consider learning more about the place itself. If you're reading this *before* you travel, find a book written about where you're traveling. The book could be a work of fiction set in that place, or it could be non-fiction.

Fiction books set in a destination can be fun to read, especially when you can visit the real-life locations described in the book. Reading a

Dan Brown thriller set in Florence, then seeing the actual locations, can bring the book to life.

If you select a non-fiction book, you might combine your hobbies or interests with that place. If you fancy yourself a chef and you're going to Italy, find a book on regional Italian cooking. If you're a historian, find a book about the history of the place you're visiting.

57. DUOLINGO FREE AD HERE. If you're traveling to a foreign country where they speak a different language, consider learning it. "Learn an entire language?" you might ask. Okay, obviously you won't have time to become fluent, unless your vacation is in like five years. However, what you can do is learn a few easy phrases.

For example, learn how to order coffee in a restaurant or ask how much something costs. Or maybe just learn how to say hello, goodbye, and thank you. Perhaps the most useful phrase, aside from "double espresso please," is "How do you say...?" or "What is the word for...?" Use these phrases your whole trip and feel slightly more like a local.

58. J'AIME LE CINEMA. Watch a movie or TV show set in your destination. This can be especially fun if the movie was filmed on location. This may be easier to do before your vacation, though you could download a movie to your computer and watch it on the plane.

59. EXTRA! EXTRA! Once on vacation, pick up a newspaper from the place you're visiting. Browse through the pages and see what's of interest to the people who live there. Even if the paper's in another language, you'll get a sense of the day based on pictures and headlines. If you can read it, see what issues matter. Whether it's politics, sports, or entertainment, you can learn a lot from the local paper.

KIDS VARIATION ON #58: Cut out pictures from the paper and bring them home to share with friends and school. Please do be sure to buy the newspaper copy before you cut out pictures. Bonus: your kids may have never actually seen a newspaper, so you can tell them this is how people got their news before TikTok.

60. FREE HBO! If you have a television in your room, flip on the set and see what people in this destination watch. But don't watch the satellite feed of cable news back home. Rather, try to find a location station and see what their programming is like. Please note I'm NOT

telling you to go on vacation and watch TV. Nope! But I do think it's interesting to see what people in your destination watch.

For example, I assume many countries have their own version of *Wheel of Fortune* or *Dancing With The Stars*. If so, who's their Vanna White? Who are their amateur dancing stars? If you can find a local news broadcast, even better. Watching the top story and one or two commercials will give you an interesting sense of the place. (Side note, in case you're puzzling over the meaning of "FREE HBO!", that was a thing in the 1970s, when motels would lure you in with the promise of watching the premium cable service, for FREE!)

61. OPEN YOUR WALLET. If you're in a destination where you carry foreign currency, learn about the denominations you have in your wallet. What's a common bill in this country? What's their equivalent of a U.S. $1 or $20 bill? If there are leaders on the bills, learn what you can about them. For example, if a visitor to the United States asked you about the "guy on the $1 bill," you could tell them it's George Washington, the guy from *Hamilton* who left in the second act to the delight of King George. See how educational money can be?

62. SUMMER SCHOOL. If you're dealing with foreign currencies, teach your kids about the exchange rate concept. Tell them $1 U.S. equals a certain amount in the other country. If they're able, ask them to do the math in their head. If the exchange rate is roughly 1:1, this is easy. If it's harder, just ask a question like, "If I have 25 Euros, does that equal more dollars or less?" (*More* at the time of publishing.)

63. ASK "WHY?" When I visit someplace new, I find myself asking "Why..." I'm curious about why things are the way they are. "Why is this hotel located here?" "Why is this street so busy?" "Why is the center of town on the river?" Asking why about things often leads to surprising details about the destination, its history, and culture.

THIS PLACE IS SO INTERESTING!

64. FIRST IMPRESSIONS. Since we're talking about the place you're visiting, let's focus on what makes it unique. Before you go any further, take three minutes and write down your first impressions of this destination. When you arrived, what did you notice? What were the sights, sounds, and smells? Think back to what stood out to you.

65. SAME AS... Looking around, and thinking back over the last 24 hours, make a list of three things that are the same as at home. Look at categories like sounds, colors, cars, street signs, homes, clothing, building styles, windows, weather, and even doorknobs! What things are the same?

66. DIFFERENT THAN... Now make a list of three things that are different. One big difference can be what kind of cars are popular in a certain place, especially if you're in a foreign country. I remember driving on the highway in Milan, Italy, and being struck by how small the cars were. The largest vehicles were smaller than mid-size cars at home. Look around and find things that are substantially different from your life back home.

67. KIDS' TURN. Ask your kids to come up with three things that are the same and three things that are different. Compare observations. Young kids especially are insightful with what they notice, so don't be surprised by the quality of their observations. If you're not keeping some kind of journal, I highly encourage you to write down what your kids share. You'll appreciate later in life being able to go back and see what they thought about the trip.

68. WHAT WOULD YOU BRING HOME? Is there a custom, food, standard, or tradition in your vacation destination you wish you had at a home? That's easy for me. When in Hawaii I love drinking Hawaiian Sun's Passion-Orange-Guava juice. If I could bring cases of that home in my suitcase, I would. So when I'm there, it makes me appreciate it all the more. What things have you experienced that you wish you could pack in your suitcase?

69. THE KIDS' POV. Ask your kids the same question. Is there something about this place they liked so much they wish you had it back home? If you get an obvious answer like "the beach," ask them "what else?" Dig deeper. Discuss what life at home would be like if they could bring things back. This is a great opportunity to learn more about what catches their attention.

70. DOCUMENT YOUR TRIP. Often, we travel to a place, spend a week there, then when we return home, someone asks a question about the destination. Things like "How many pools were there?" "How long did it take to get from your hotel to the cafe?" or "How long was the beach?" One way to enhance your sense of observation

is to choose a few interesting things to document. Find something of interest to you and be observant about it. If you love that little boulangerie, count how many types of pastries they carry. How many floors does your hotel have? How many steps can you take into the ocean before you reach waist-deep water? Yes, these may be trivial things. But if they interest you, and cause you to pay attention, great!

71. YOUR VACATION TOP TEN. Create your own Top Ten List of things you like about this destination or this trip. It can be physical features, great experiences, wonderful meals, kind people who helped you, or whatever stands out. Write this list in your vacation journal. Compile your list during the week, adding 3–4 favorites per day. At the end of the week, reduce the list down to your top ten.

72. THE LOCAL CUSTOMS. Learn one interesting custom of your destination. It might be the dress, time to eat, morning beverage, popular music, whatever fascinates you. We're used to our ways of doing things, so it can be illuminating to see differences around the world. For example, we might drink coffee or tea in the morning, so you could make it your mission to find out what's the most popular morning beverage on your vacation.

73. PICK ONE THING. Learn what you can about one building, piece of art, or another culturally significant landmark. Discover enough so you could "teach" someone else. Let's say I'm in Hawaii, and I see a statue of Duke Kahanamoku. I notice tourists drape leis around his bronze statue. Curious about this, I Google info and learn the lei placement custom is thought to hasten your return to Hawaii. I then share this info with one of my traveling companions. I ask them to find out something else and share that with me.

74. WHAT'S THE OLDEST THING? If you're in a place with unique history, play a game where you search for the oldest building, monument, or structure. Google "Oldest .... in .... " Whoever finds the oldest one wins. This can be a great way to engage kids in the destination, but it's good for adults too. Because now you are more likely to check out the guidebook or go online and learn what you can about each place you see.

75. CHILDLIKE WONDER. Ask your kids what they're curious about, then go with them to discover the answer. For example, if your kids were enamored of the penguins at the Hilton Hawaiian Village in

Waikiki, help them learn more. Where do the penguins sleep at night? What do they eat? Is it ever too hot for them? Where does this species normally live? Ask your kids what THEY want to know, then lead them on a journey to discover the answers.

76. CARTOGRAPHY. If you have even the slightest bit of artistic skill, draw a map of where you are staying. On your drawing, note things of interest in your location. For example, if you're staying in Rome, Italy, draw a map of where your hotel is relative to interesting sites. Note marks for your favorite cafe, that museum you loved, or the street where you saw that funny street performer. The act of drawing a map causes you to be more observant of your setting and engages your curiosity about the sights.

77. HEY, PICASSO! If you're comfortable creating a map, why not stretch your artistic talent and pick something in your vacation setting to draw? Keep it simple. Maybe sketch a tree, a sign, a sunset. If it helps, trace an existing piece of art. You can also use a computer tablet to help create art. No matter your skill level, have fun!

78. LIKE THE BACK OF YOUR HAND? If you're in a familiar destination you know like the back of your hand, try the same exercise above. Pretend that this week was your first time here. Pick 1–2 of the activities above and do one today.

It's easy to go on autopilot when you're in the same old place. We know our way around so we do the same things. We have our favorite haunts, and we always eat or drink in the same places. But what if you didn't? For just one day, forget what you think you know and see this place with new eyes.

79. GET OUTDOORS. Find a local park or outdoor venue and spend time there. Perhaps there's a garden nearby. Take a towel and a book and claim your space and enjoy the day. You might also get curious about the park. What type of visitors come here? Why is the space designed the way it is? If this area has a particular history, as parks in big cities often do, research that.

80. GO SHOPPING! "Finally!" you say, travel advice you can use! Though this is shopping with a twist. Instead of a quest to load yourself up with shopping bags, why not focus on having a unique experience.

If you come across a shop that specializes in a specific product, wander around and learn what you can.

For example, you might find a guitar shop in Barcelona or a blown-glass shop in Venice. You might not be in the market for either of these, but you could window shop and learn more, such as how they're made, the history behind them, what's the most popular, or whatever else the shop proprietor might share with you.

THE PEOPLE HERE ARE SO INTERESTING

81. CHECK OUT THE LOCALS. Try to learn what you can about the people who live here. We travel to far-off destinations and interact with people who serve us. Why not get to know them?

Get curious about the people who live where you are visiting. It might be someone at your hotel or resort, on the ship, or at a tourist site you're visiting. Pick one person today, and ask about their experience living here. Consider questions like:

- Did they grow up here?
- What's their favorite season?
- What's one of the biggest holidays here?
- What's a benefit to living here?
- What's a challenge to living here?
- Where's one of the most popular areas to live?

82. TELL ME ABOUT YOUR JOB. Another way to learn about people is to ask them about their job. How many days a week do they work? How many hours a day? How far do they live from work? What is their career path? What's considered a good job in their field? If they weren't doing this job, what else might they be interested in? What are the benefits of this job? What are the challenges? Showing genuine interest in their work is something they probably don't often see.

83. WHERE DO THE LOCALS HANG OUT? If you're in a touristy area, you are not getting a genuine sense of the destination. Main Street at Disneyland is not how people in Southern California live (unless you're a six-foot-tall mouse named Mickey.) If possible (and safe) look for the places locals hang out. If you're in a beach-type destination, ask what beach they prefer. If you're in a foreign city, ask what restaurants, shops, or cafes the locals frequent.

84. EAT LIKE A LOCAL. Find a restaurant where locals frequent. You could ask a server who's helping you (who you trust), "Where do you eat?" or "What's a place tourists don't know about?" If you have concerns about the area, ask the hotel desk or concierge for advice. Emphasize you want to go somewhere easy to get to, and also safe.

85. WHERE DO *YOU* SPEND YOUR LEISURE TIME? For the people who live and work where you're on vacation, this may be their home, even if temporarily. Find out where they spend their time off.

Ask three people where they go in their leisure time. Ask what they like about it and if they would recommend it. A follow-up question could be to ask what's the one place they've always wanted to visit, and why. (Side note: don't be surprised if people you speak with don't necessarily enjoy vacations or holidays the way many westerners do. They may take breaks to travel or sightseeing, but if you're an hourly worker, your "time off" may be enjoyed in more modest ways.)

86. ONE "MUST-SEE" IS... Ask a local what's one thing you must know about their home. If they could only recommend one sight to see, what would it be? If it's not on your list, consider adding it.

87. IF YOU HAD ONE DAY. Another way to explore your destination through the eyes of your host is to ask them how they would spend one day here. "If I only had one day to spend in .... , how would you spend it? What would you see or do?" The obvious intent here is to ask for their advice on what *you* should do. But you may find interesting perspectives by asking what *they* would do with 24 hours to do anything they want.

THE ROAD LESS TRAVELED

88. BE DARING. Is there something you've always wanted to try? A vacation can be the perfect opportunity to try things you've never done before. Let's say you've always wanted to do stand-up paddle boarding. If your hotel or resort has that sport, try it! If you like it, you'll have additional time to practice and improve your skills. What kinds of things could you try? Many all-inclusive resorts offer activities like scuba, sailing, wind surfing, snorkeling and golf. If it's included, and you could do as much as you'd like, why not try it?

89. START ON THE LOW DIVE. You're ready to try something new. Great! But what? Maybe you're not ready to jump off the high dive

— something that either might scare you, or be a significant time or cost investment. If so, start with the "low dive" to ease your way in. For example, learning scuba might be your high dive. It could take an entire week and could be costly. But you could start on the low dive and go on a snorkeling trip. Or maybe you're a golfer, but you don't want to invest the time and money playing 18 holes. If so, see if you could try out the putting green. Or maybe your "high dive" is an adventurous new cuisine. If so, start with a tapas-sized appetizer.

90. BLAZE NEW TRAILS. If you know this place well — perhaps because it's your regular vacation destination — consider going beyond the familiar. Avoid routine and habit. This advice can apply even in situations where, mid-vacation, you might find yourself falling into a routine. If you find yourself taking the same route, elevator, path, spot on the beach, or seat in the cafe, allow yourself to make discoveries and new things. Have fun with unpredictability.

91. HIT THE ROAD. Rent a car at your destination and spend time exploring, assuming it's safe. If you have questions, ask your hotel, concierge, or travel adviser where to go and what to see. With smartphone apps and inexpensive data plans, it's hard these days to get lost. A favorite memory of visiting the Greek island of Corfu was driving across the island to a less-crowded beach. We passed road signs written in a completely different alphabet and wondered what they said. Our conclusion: "It's all Greek to me."

92. TAKE THE "A" TRAIN. If you're in a place where it's not practical to rent a car, take the bus, train, or subway to your excursion. Guidebooks on your destination can give you advice on how to use public transportation and whether it's advisable in this location. Certainly, this would be easier to do in a place where you are comfortable with the language. While on the bus or train, be curious about the people around you. What do they have in common? How do riders compare to public transportation at home?

93. JOIN THE CIRCUS. If you can participate in a show at your hotel, resort, or ship, do it! Be the guest who gets called onto the stage to participate. Whether it's a dating gameshow, a skill contest, or getting pulled into a dance, be open to participating. After all, the people who get pulled on stage look like they're having fun, don't they?

94. ONE WORD A DAY. If you're in a place with a different language, build your language skills by learning one new word a day (or more, if you're feeling ambitious.) How to do this without a guidebook? Easy. Pick any object nearby. It could be a chair, a cup, a plate, a type of food, a tree, or even a pigeon. Approach a friendly-looking local, point to the bird, and ask (in their language), "What is the word for..." (Google this phrase in advance.) If possible, ask them how to spell the word. Make sure to thank them, in their language, of course. If you keep a journal, write down your newfound words.

95. "I WOULD NEVER EAT THAT." Is there a food you're curious about? Or something you could never imagine yourself eating? Well, you guessed it, you're going to try it. Just one thing. Maybe you are in France, and you see escargot on the menu. Yes, snails. For the longest time, I vowed I would never eat this dish. Until the night I dared myself. You know what? I kind of liked it!

This is an especially good thing to do if you're in a destination that has a signature dish or food. Or if you're in an all-inclusive resort, this should almost be a requirement. After all, everything's included. If you don't like something, hey, at least you tried it, and it didn't cost you anything. If it gives you the motivation to get through this, do a little humble bragging on social media, and impress your friends with how adventurous you are.

96. KIDS! EAT DESSERT FIRST! If you're traveling as a family, pick a night to let the kids choose the order of your meal courses. This typically works well for dinner. If they want to eat dessert first, let them. Or if it's possible to order breakfast for dinner, go for it.

97. CHECK OUT THE MENU. Go to the most expensive or exclusive restaurant you can find, order the cheapest thing on the menu, then stay as long as you can. Note this may not always be practical. You may have to sit at the bar. You may have to nurse a glass of wine. The point is to push yourself beyond your comfort zone. If you're like me and don't want to be rude or break norms, this may not be easy, which is probably why you should try it! At the same time, please be respectful of the establishment and your server.

98. ASK IF YOU CAN TRY. If you feel a little daring, ask if you can participate in an activity. For example, if you're a musician, ask the local hotel band if you can sit in with them for a set, or sing a song

when it isn't karaoke night. Of course, it's probably best to do this only if you can play an instrument or sing a song and know the lyrics. Other ways to make your experience interactive include asking the bartender if you can wield the mojito shaker or asking the bakery if you can put the tray of croissants into the oven. Hint: if asking to join scares you, that's even more reason to consider it.

99. BREAK OUT THE TUX? Look for opportunities to enjoy a cultural or civic activity. This could be a musical performance, art exhibition, stage show, museum exhibit, or civic parade. How would you discover these? Often your hotel concierge will have an exploration guide, with local events listed by date. You can also Google a term like "What's going on." Of course, a tuxedo or formal dress should be considered very optional — you're on vacation!

100. FIND A STREET FAIR. Ask your hotel if there's a street fair or farmers market nearby. If it's close to where you're staying, this can be a fun way to shop like a local and see what's common during the season you're there. The food you find at a farmers market can be an especially good opportunity to try something new ("That's a fruit? Really?") You'll also find lots of colorful photo opportunities.

101. DO THE (VERY) UNEXPECTED. If you're in Paris, of course, you're going to visit the Louvre. If you're in London, you'll see London Bridge. But why not balance these must-see museums or sites with something less well-known? In Paris, you could visit the Paris Sewer Museum (seriously, that's for real.) In London, you can check out the Museum of Crime at New Scotland Yard where you'll see items used by Jack the Ripper. You can find these offbeat sites by Googling "Weird .... Museums in .... " with the name of your destination.

102. TAILGATE TIME! Attend a local sporting event. If you're in a place where it's possible to enjoy a sports match or game, consider this a way to enjoy local culture. I'm not suggesting you search for pricey NFL or World Cup tickets. Rather, if there's a cricket match or a minor league game, this can be a fun way to live like a local.

103. TAKE A CLASS. Almost anywhere you travel, you're likely to find a class in the arts, music, or culinary fields. Often this might be through your hotel, resort, or ship. Ask the concierge what's available. Classes could include cooking, glass blowing, drink mixology, wine pairing,

Hawaiian lei making, dress-sewing, painting, sculpture, hairweaving, or horticulture.

104. GET SPIRITUAL. If you attend a denominational service at home, consider visiting a local church, synagogue, or mosque for service on vacation. If you're in Italy, for example, many local churches welcome guests to their services, though you may want to confirm service times in advance, as well as dress codes. A good concierge can help with this.

BE PREPARED TO SHARE

105. WHAT I DID THIS SUMMER. In grade school, one of the first activities you did in the fall was share what you did over the summer. You reported on something you did, a place you visited, or people you met. As adults, we don't do this anymore. Aside from sharing photos of our travels on social media, we don't return home and tell people about what we did. Consider changing that.

Decide that upon returning home, you will give a five-minute talk to someone about your travels. It doesn't have to be elaborate. Five minutes is basically long enough for you to share three brief observations about the things you did or learned. Review the lists you made and think about the people you spoke with. Now choose three things you want to share.

106. WRITTEN BY... If you want to take your sharing a step further, imagine you were a travel book writer. Your job is to describe the destination in a way that paints a picture of the place and excites the imagination of a reader. Consider writing a brief article about your trip. Describe as much as you can in your piece. When you return home, find a way to share. Post on Facebook or a site like Medium.

107. YOUR INNER HEMINGWAY. If you really want to stretch your creativity, write a short story set in this destination. It could be a simple premise you bring alive because of your knowledge of the destination. For example, your story's protagonist could be a young woman waiting for someone in a French cafe. Who is she waiting for? Why is she there? What will happen in this meeting? Those would be the questions your short story would answer. The details you share of her experience — the taste of her coffee, the sounds of the street, the things she sees — these would all be the elements you can observe

while you're in this destination. Your first-hand experience will give the writing an authenticity you can only get by being in that location.

108. A FILM BY...YOU! Take out that movie studio you have in your pocket that is your phone and create a mini-documentary of your destination. Capture short pieces of video footage of things that interest you. You can even provide your own narration. "This is our hotel." "Here's where we ate." "Here's a museum we saw." "Here's our beach." "Here's a town on the river." "This is my favorite. drink." You get the idea. Don't overthink it or worry too much about technical polish. If you create a movie with 20 scenes from your vacation, you'll go home with a unique souvenir of your experience (more on souvenirs later in Chapter 5.)

109. BECOME AN EXPERT. If you're vacationing in a destination with a famous landmark, learn three facts about it. You might visit the Grand Canyon, Victoria Falls, the Panama Canal, Seattle's Space Needle, the Eiffel Tower, or the Pyramids of Giza. If so, look for three interesting facts you can take home and share with others. One way to do this is to ask the tour guide or docent, "What's something people are surprised to learn?"

110. KIDS SHARE THE DARNDEST THINGS. If you're traveling with children, help them decide what they want to share about their vacation experience. Encourage them to write things down. If they don't write, or if they are more artistic, maybe they could draw pictures about something they like. If you did this for every vacation experience they have had over the years, and you saved them all in a scrapbook, imagine what a treasure this would be.

3

PAMPER YOUR WELL-BEING

55 Practices to Renew, Recharge & Relax

You're on vacation! Woo hoo! Live it up! Partay! "Thor," you might say, "I'm already doing that. I don't need to be reminded to enjoy my vacation." Well, yes, that's true for most of us. We know what to do on vacation. We know how to eat and drink. And eat and drink. And eat and drink — yes, I get it. We know how to enjoy ourselves.

There's a reason why all-inclusive vacations are so popular. They give us an unlimited variety and volume of food and beverages we may not have at home. We don't have to think about what we want. We just want it, we ask for it, and we get it. It's a beautiful thing.

"Oh no, I can see the lesson coming from a mile away," you may be thinking. "He's gonna tell me I shouldn't indulge, I should be better, I should be stronger."

Not exactly.

Well, yes, sort of.

Actually, today I want you to be more considerate of yourself. Considerate in the sense of being kind to yourself; considerate in the deliberate sense, meaning, consider what you're doing. Take care of yourself by being more aware of what you're choosing and doing.

Today is about three things: renewing, recharging, and yes, relaxing.

Most of us *think* we know how to relax. It usually involves alcohol, a beach chair, and lots of shuteye. Those can be good things, in moderation, assuming we choose those things consciously.

You might decide, for example, that you really want that 16 oz. craft brew while relaxing by the pool (or, even better, relaxing *in* the pool.) And that's fine. But before you order it, you might stop, pause, and ask yourself, "Do I want this drink? Am I going to appreciate it? Will I focus on the consumption of it?" In other words, ask yourself, *"Why do I want this?"*

Sometimes we make these decisions in a non-deliberate way. We might do it because we see other people doing it, and without thinking, we join in.

For example, I might see others eating or drinking something — a beer, a glass of wine, that yummy dessert, that plate of nachos — and without thinking, I order it. I'm not connected to a deeper reason. I'm not thinking of the benefits or the consequences of doing it.

Occasionally that's okay. Part of being on vacation is disconnecting from having to always think about consequences. We want to live. We want to be. We want to do. We want to defer worrying about everything until tomorrow. We've all said this. At least, I know I have. A certain amount of this attitude is understandable. We work hard when we're at home. We need some time off.

Just for a moment, let's add another viewpoint to this discussion. I'm not saying we can't relax in our normal ways (eating, drinking, sleeping.) Rather, let's think about relaxing in a more deliberate way.

For example, take renewal. "Ahh," you might be thinking. "Renewing must somehow be connected to visiting the spa." You're right. It is! See, I'm not all about deprivation. You should enjoy the experience of being on vacation. And there's no better way to do this than to treat yourself to something you might not do at home. Nurture yourself.

You might decide, for example, to get a massage. Or have your nails done. Or relax in the sauna. While doing any of these things, remember to be connected to the moment. As you're having the massage, or as you sit in the sauna, allow yourself to enjoy it. Think about *why* you deserve this. Permit yourself to enjoy the moment.

We also want to define "renewal" as more than just treating yourself. Think of renewal as nourishing your mind and body. Consider making choices consistent with your best interest.

Be more aware of your environment, your routines, and your choices. You might decide to omit some of those choices today, just for the day, and notice how you feel about that.

Finally, the third area I suggest you focus on is recharging — bringing a new sense of vigor and vitality into your life. There are many ways to do this, both for the mind and body. We'll talk more about them in this chapter, but one of the easiest ways to do this is to introduce some physical activity into your day.

Make sense? Relax, renew and recharge. Today, pick one activity from each of those three categories (Yes, I know I'm suggesting more than two.) You don't have to do them in order. But because making conscious choices is one of the themes of the day, if possible, decide early on which activities appeal to you most. Have fun with the day!

RELAX, YOU'RE ON VACATION

111. START BY DOING LESS. EXACTLY ONE THING LESS. When people go on vacation, they often try to cram as much as they can into the 1–2 weeks they have, which leads to returning home to a chorus of "I need a vacation from my vacation." Instead, dial back on the activities.

Just for one day, decide you won't do quite as much. Leave yourself time to do nothing at all. What will you do with this time? Nothing! No, I'm kidding. Don't do anything. Rather, do one less thing. If you would normally do 4–5 things in a day, do 3–4. Give yourself more breathing room in the activities you choose.

For example, instead of rushing through several museums on a day in London or New York, maybe visit one less place, but spend more time in each one. Give yourself a more relaxed agenda, and you may enjoy your activities more.

112. DO NOTHING FOR A CHANGE. How long can you just sit in one place? Most of us have a difficult time with this. We're always on the move, doing things, going places, and accomplishing tasks. But since you're on vacation, maybe you could, oh, I don't know, let yourself get bored. You read that right.

Today, pick a moment and just let yourself get bored. Do nothing for ten minutes. Maybe you're sitting on the beach, looking at the water. A thought occurs to you to grab a book or go in the water. Resist that notion for ten minutes. Instead, just sit there. Maybe look around. Notice things. Listen. Watch. Process. For just ten minutes. When time's up, write down your experience of unplugging.

113. SIESTA TIME. Do you take naps at home? "Sleep during the day?" you ask. "That's crazy talk!" Well, you're on vacation, and I'm going to propose something completely radical. Take a nap. But not just any nap. Take one where you don't set the alarm on your phone. Maybe you already do this. That's great. But many people will only allow themselves to nap if they know they'll get back to work in a set period, like 20 or 30 minutes. That's fine for home. But not on vacation. If the mood strikes you today, take a siesta free of any alarms.

114. FLOATING ALONG. If you can float on a raft, do it. Whether it's in the pool, ocean, or a river, floating along with your eyes closed, listening to the sound of water, the warm feeling of the sun on your skin, *mmmm*, this is true relaxation. I think this is now one of my mottos in life: when you have the chance to float, do it!

115. KIDS LOVE TO FLOAT! If you have more than one raft, float with your kids. Position your rafts side-by-side, a hand gently holding onto them, and just drift where you may. P.S., this works well with your spouse too.

116. ENJOY YOUR MEALS MORE. Many people go on vacation to do as many things as possible, and mealtime is no exception. Do you find yourself rushing through meals? That's understandable when you're at home and you're busy living your life. But on vacation, you can presumably give yourself more time. Today, pick one meal and decide you will spend at least twice as much time as you would at home

enjoying your food. Yes, that's right, twice as much time. If an average dinner at home is 30 minutes, spend 60 minutes on a vacation dinner.

117. SLOW DOWN AND CHEW YOUR FOOD. You might wonder how you could possibly spend 60 minutes in one sitting. How can this possibly be done? Easy. Pace yourself. Slow down. Put your fork down in between each bite and gradually chew your food. Crazy, right?

118. THIS TASTES INCREDIBLE. You can also be more present by noticing the tastes of your food. Slow down as you eat. Enjoy each bite. Savor the food. Be present at that moment. If you're in a beautiful setting, connect the food to the environment. Imagine a bite of perfectly grilled steak or salmon, savored while looking at the sunset. If you're traveling with others, encourage them to join in. You could all take a bite of food at the same time, after which you share your individual impressions. Not only will you enjoy the food more, but you'll be more connected to your dining companions.

119. "HOW WAS YOUR DAY?" Another way to enjoy a more deliberate meal is to engage your dining companions in a little thing we used to call "conversation." Sadly, we don't do this so much anymore, but when you're on vacation, it's a perfect opportunity to share, discuss and learn. We'll expand more on this in a later chapter, but for now, consider posing this one question at a meal: What was your favorite thing today?

120. DRINK MORE WATER. No matter how much water you drink at home, decide you will drink more on vacation. If you normally carry a plastic water bottle, you have a handy measuring device. If you refill it 2–3 times at home, why not increase that to 3–4 times on vacation? If you don't already have a bottle, you can probably find a souvenir version and begin today.

121. TRY THE SPA WATER, DARLING. Maybe plain water isn't your thing, and the thought of drinking 3–4 bottles a day is inconceivable to you. If so, consider making your own spa water. If you have access to any kind of fruit, especially tropical, make your own. What works well? Strawberries, kiwis, orange slices, or lemons. Add a cucumber from the salad bar. You could also stop by the hotel or ship bar and ask for a sprig of mint. Add your ingredients to a thermos full of water and ice, and voilà! Instant spa water!

122. SAVOR THE SIP. Not only can we be more thoughtful with our meals, but we can also do so with our drinking. Yes, I mean alcohol. If you don't partake, skip this. If you do, and you've been known to consume just a little more while on vacation, consider being more deliberate with your consumption just for this one day.

What does that look like? Simple. Each time you take a sip of your drink, whether it's beer, wine, or a mai tai, think about nothing else but that sip. Notice the taste of the beverage. Each sip. Take several seconds to appreciate it, then put the drink down. I can't say if this more relaxed approach to consumption will cause you to drink less, but you'll certainly appreciate your drink more.

123. AN APPLE A DAY. Snack on a piece of fruit today. If you're in a destination where the in-season, locally-grown fruit is abundant, like pineapple in Hawaii, this should be a no-brainer. Most beach destinations generally have tropical fruit selections. If you're in a city like Lisbon or Venice, seek out a fruit stand and ask the vendor what's the freshest in-season fruit available. Snack on that. Bonus points if you seek out a fruit you've never tried before (for me, this would be a kumquat. Where do you even find those?)

TIME TO RENEW

124. START SIMPLE. Today can be a day to take care of yourself, and there are many ways you can do that. If you have decided to treat yourself on this vacation, make today that day. Start with one of the most simple things you can do: drink more water. Start with one glass. Like right now. Drink up! (There, you did it! *Right?*)

125. PAMPER YOURSELF. You might decide to get a massage or other kind of personal treatment like a facial, manicure, or pedicure. And gentlemen, you don't have to feel left out. Many resorts have versions of all these treatments just for guys. While doing any of these, remember to connect to the moment.

As you have the massage, or as you sit in the sauna, allow yourself to savor the experience. Think about why you deserve this. Permit yourself to enjoy the moment. Now, many people arrive at their hotel, resort, or ship intending to get a massage, but they see the prices and say, "That's more than I'd pay at home!" Resist this notion. I'm not suggesting you disregard cost. Not at all. Rather, I recommend you consider value. Speaking of which...

126. A MASSAGE IN NATURE. If the spa treatment opportunity you have is unique — for example, a beachside massage, a manicure overlooking the ocean, or a facial with Hawaiian products — consider it an experience you can't have at home. Thought of that way, the additional cost may be worth it.

127. WILL YOU BE MY MASSEUSE? Maybe you don't have the opportunity to get a professional massage. But if you're traveling with a spouse or friend, you could ask them to be your masseuse. Even a simple five-minute back rub can do wonders. Offer to give one in return. And hey, if you have to apply sunscreen, turn it into a mini-backrub session.

128. BARTER WITH THE KIDS. Ask for a back massage from your kids in exchange for doing something for them. Of course, the quality of their massage may not be what you'd get from your spouse, but their sweetness might make up for it. And chances are, you probably would've done that thing for them anyway. This way, you get a nice mini-massage in return.

129. YOUR BODY IS YOUR TEMPLE. Another way to take care of the body is to deliberately choose what you put into it. Daily, we have stimulants we take in — things like coffee, alcohol, and even media or the news. Those substances change how we feel. So for one day, why not consider cutting out just one of those things and noticing what effect it has. Take coffee, for example. Most of us know how caffeine deprivation can affect us. Headaches, lethargy, lack of focus. Have you experienced this? Consider finding out.

Now, you might say, I don't want caffeine withdrawal headaches on vacation. Fair enough, and honestly, I agree with you. So maybe consider drinking one cup of coffee for the day, enough to stave off the headache. You could also limit or curtail your alcohol intake. Substitute something such as mineral water, or a flavored non-alcoholic drink unique to your destination. Relax, it's just for one day. Remember, you're a temple. A damn fine one!

130. CUT OUT ONE OF THESE. Just for today, drop sugar or wheat from your diet. See how you feel as a result. I know this doesn't sound

like fun. No sugar means no desserts. No wheat means no pastries or fresh-baked baguettes. Okay, now I'm starting to talk myself out of this idea. No, wait! I mean it! It's only one day. You might discover you can live without it. Or not, and that's fine too.

131. SLIP INTO THE TUB. If your room has a soaking tub, give yourself the gift of a relaxing bath. At home, we probably view the shower or tub as part of our daily routine. We have to take a shower or bath to get our day started. Now that you are on vacation, why not take a bath simply for sheer pleasure. Just like characters do in Shonda Rhimes TV shows. Get yourself some candles, and a glass of wine, turn on the hot water, and enjoy a little "me time." Or if it's appropriate, maybe turn it into "us time." (P.S "us time" does NOT mean kids. That was clear, right?) (Also to be clear: "slip" in the tub meant relax into it. Don't slip and fall.)

132. INDULGE YOUR SWEET TOOTH. Let's say you're in a destination famous for its confectionery treats. Maybe just this once, allow yourself to enjoy a local treat. Okay, I know I just suggested cutting out sugar for a day but hear me out. First, you don't have to do that one. Second, I'm not suggesting you go to town on a bag of Snickers, unless you happen to be vacationing in the hometown of Snickers. Nor am I suggesting you order a scone from the Starbucks in Costa Rica. No.

What I am suggesting is, if you're in Switzerland, a little authentic swiss dark chocolate might be okay. One beignet in New Orleans isn't a sweet indulgence, it's a culinary exploration. Find a local treat, then feel good about trying it. When you do, savor it. Be in the moment. Let there be nothing else but you and that chocolate.

133. "KIDS, WE'RE GETTING A SITTER." Get a sitter for the kids one night. Hopefully in a different room from you and your spouse. Trust me, you'll find ways to occupy yourself for two hours. Maybe it's all this talk about hot baths, candles, and dark chocolate. But if it's been forever since you've had some "alone time," it's your right and privilege as parents to take one evening (or afternoon) just for you.

134. JOIN S.M.A. (SOCIAL MEDIA ANONYMOUS) "Hi, I'm Thor and I'm addicted to social media." There, that wasn't so hard, was it? Some of us may find ourselves spending too much time on social media. So when it comes to vacation, another thing to consider adding to the detox list is time spent on your phone checking the socials. What's interesting about the internet and vacation is that the two did not co-exist ten years ago. It used to be when you went on vacation, you didn't have your phone with you, or if you did, you put it in the safe for the duration of your stay.

Now whether you are on a ship, at a tropical resort, or in a foreign country, chances are you'll have easy access to the internet. You can share your status, check updates, and post drink and food pictures. But just because you can doesn't mean you have to. Why not take a break from social media for one day? Don't post anything today about your trip. The crazy idea coming here — why not just leave your phone in the safe? Today only, relax. I know it's your camera now too. Tomorrow, first thing, you can post how virtuous you were for staying off social media for 24 hours.

135. I HEARD THE NEWS TODAY, OH BOY. Let me ask you a question. If a news story falls in the woods, and you're not around to witness it, did it still happen? Yes. And who cares? Have you ever gone a whole day where you didn't check on the day's headlines? Maybe you're not much of a news or sports junkie. But if you're a "must-know-it-all," consider going without your fix today. Unless you are the leader of a country or CEO of a global behemoth, chances are very good the world can carry on nicely without you knowing every detail of its affairs. Your ball team will still win or lose even if you aren't updated on the score. Again, putting your phone in the safe is the best way to keep yourself from falling prey to the news-fix habit.

136. "OMMMMM..." At this point, you might be thinking, what am I going to do with all this free time? After all, you're cutting out all these other activities, what will take their place? Several possibilities. If you've never tried meditating before, vacation is a great place to start. Take 5 or 10 minutes, find a quiet place you won't be disturbed, sit down, close your eyes, and simply focus on something like your breath. If a thought occurs to you, notice that you are noticing it, and then let go of the thought as if it were a cloud.

If you could hear my voice now, it would be soothing and melodious. Yes, you'll have thoughts coming and going from your mind. That's normal. Just note them and release them. Maybe measure how many breaths you can take before a thought pops into your mind. Count your inhaled breaths, 1–2–3, etc., and see how far you can go before a thought appears. That's all there is to it. If this seems challenging, find a smartphone app that makes the process simple. I like the Calm app. When you meditate in paradise, you may hear sounds like ocean waves, just like on the app. Why not enjoy the real thing? [Okay soothing and melodious voice ending now.]

137. SIT FOR A BIT. (Hey, that rhymes. I love things like that on vacation, don't you?) If meditation isn't your thing, you could sit somewhere quiet and listen to the sounds of nature. Close your eyes. Or don't. But be mindful of your senses. What do you hear? What senses do you feel? Are there any interesting smells? Take in everything, notice it, then let it go. Oh wait, were your eyes closed? You might have almost meditated. If so, well done. And if that didn't seem so bad, consider going back to #136 above.

138. ZONE OUT. You could approximate a meditative state by picking an object to stare at, then just zoning out. Notice what you can about this object. Try not to think of anything else but the object. Many meditation practices have us focus on the breath. Here, you're putting your attention on something you can see. If you're at the beach or on the ocean, you could stare at the waves or the horizon. If the water shimmers, maybe fixate on the word "shimmer." Hold that thought and just relax.

139. CONE OF SILENCE. Another way to get out of your head is to stop talking. Just stop talking. No, not forever, but for a short period. If you're traveling with others, this might work better if you tell people in advance. "Mommy is taking a break from talking for half an hour. I'll be back soon, okay?" What will you do when you're not talking? You might take in your environment. Make notes about what you see. Listen to what you hear. Ask yourself (internally, of course) questions about what you notice. And enjoy the silence.

140. "KIDS, LET'S PLAY A GAME." If you're a parent, this one idea might be worth the entire price of the book. What about doing #139 with your kids. Tell them "Cone of Silence" is a game and ask them to play along. Depending on their age, you might need to shorten their period of silence. See how long they can go. Encourage them to "save up their questions." Tell them to write down their questions so they won't forget. When time's up, they can ask you everything they wrote down. Though chances are, the practice of silence might encourage them to answer their questions. By the way, you're welcome.

141. REACH OUT AND TOUCH. If you're engaging in moments of quiet, you can enhance that time by activating your sense of touch. Humans use sight and hearing the most. Touch tends to be something we engage less. But you're on vacation, so why not do something out of the ordinary? Decide that during your "Cone of Silence" time, you will simply observe how things feel. Touch plants, water, sand, grass. Notice the texture. Is it smooth, rough, soft, sticky, or slick? What's the temperature? Is it warm, cool? If you're touching a piece of paper, can you feel the texture of the print?

We think of our hands as our primary means of feeling, but of course, other parts of our body can feel sensations too. Pay attention to experiences like the sun on your skin, the wind in your air, your feet on the grass, or the way a part of your body makes contact with other objects. You may discover all sorts of new impressions by focusing more on touch.

142. WHAT'S THAT SMELL? Of course, we can't talk about sensations without mentioning smell. If you're observing a few moments of quiet, why not notice what smells and scents you can observe in your environment? This might be easy in a tropical location. You could detect the smell of plants. Or the salt air from the ocean. Or maybe the sweet sensations from a bakery. Whatever's in the air, see if you can detect it. How many different smells can you discern?

143. STOP AND SMELL THE ROSES. Seriously, just stop. Find a rose or flower in your environment. Lean over, close your eyes, and enjoy. Don't be afraid to stay awhile and just enjoy the moment.

144. PLAY SPA MUSIC. Speaking of your senses, another way you can spend the day in rejuvenation mode is to create a song playlist on your phone, one that calms and soothes your spirit. Services like Apple Music, Spotify, and Pandora all have spa-type radio stations. Maybe play one of those for an hour while staring at a scenic view. Of course, if you think having your phone in hand will cause you to want to check social media, it might not be worth bringing that temptation into your experience today. But tomorrow, who knows, maybe...

145. GET SCENTS-ABLE. Add aromatherapy to your vacation setting. We've all had the feeling — the scents-ation (okay, I'll stop with the puns now) — of walking into a spa or high-end shop and enjoying the

fragrance of the setting. Hotels like Westin use this to great effect. Their signature vanilla sandalwood scent puts me in a wonderful mood whenever I stay there. Why not create that same effect in your hotel room? Pick up a reed diffuser with a local scent and place it near your bed or in the bathroom. Hint: taking this home can remind you of vacation.

146. ORDER FLOWERS. Treat yourself to fresh flowers. In most hotels or cruise lines, you can order flowers sent to your room. Why not take advantage of this minor indulgence? I mean, you love receiving flowers at home, and you love being on vacation. Imagine if you combined both of those experiences into one. It's like the old commercial for Reese's Peanut Butter Cups. "Who put flowers in my hotel room?" "Who put a hotel room in my flowers??" Is that too much pleasure? No! And by the way, if you do have flowers in your room, every time you come or go, head over to the vase so you can, you guessed it, stop and smell the roses. Or whatever flowers you get.

147. JOURNAL IT. Write down what you're feeling about the day's experience. If you eliminated something from your day like coffee or added something like meditation, take 10 minutes and write down your thoughts. What was the experience like? What did you learn? Would you do it again? Jot down any thoughts. If you aren't a regular journal writer and you like this experience, take 5–10 minutes every evening and write down your thoughts about the day.

RECHARGING

148. GET STARTED. You're rested and relaxed. Maybe you're ready for a little recharging. If you don't regularly exercise at home, why not start now? Don't worry. "Start" doesn't have to be the beginning of anything huge. Just do something physical today. Go for a walk. Swim in the ocean. Jog through the park. Do jumping jacks on the sand, sit-ups on the grass, and pushups by the river. Any movement you add to your day can be good. A bonus to adding movement: it's easier to rationalize having that frozen tourist drink later in the day!

149. DO A LITTLE BIT MORE. If you already exercise at home, great. Your goal today is to challenge yourself. Do more than you already do. For example, if you walk or run at a certain pace, just add a little more. One more minute. A slightly faster pace. A few more crunches.

150. USE THE ENVIRONMENT. In your exercise, take advantage of your destination's unique qualities. One of the benefits of being on vacation is the location. You could try yoga at home, but yoga on the beach is even better. A brisk walk in your hometown is fine. The same walk in Rome? Historic! A swim in the pool at the Y, is nice. Swimming in the warm Caribbean at sunset, now you're talking magic. If you're in Paris, do your walk in the Tuileries Garden by the Louvre. If you're on a ship, get on the elliptical with an ocean view.

No matter where you are, you probably have access to fitness equipment or classes you don't have at home. Take advantage. Do one thing today you couldn't at home.

151. PLAY OUTDOORS WITH THE KIDDOS. Speaking of environment, if you are in a place with a beach or pool, why not enjoy that water slide or beach game with your kids. Maybe it's tossing a frisbee on the beach. Or doing that ropes course on the ship. If there's a water park where you are, do that. Bonus points for standing with your kids under that giant bucket of water that dumps hundreds of gallons every seven minutes.

152. TAKE A CLASS. If your vacation destination offers exercise classes, why not take a class or two? Some resorts include exercise classes or offer them at a reduced cost. This can be a great way to try a new activity. After all, it's close, and you don't have to worry about going back to work after. Maybe it's yoga, stretching, or dance. Or possibly a guided run or fitness boot camp workout. Do you know what's best about taking an exercise class? If you do it first thing in the morning, your breakfast tastes really amazing (because it probably now includes a piece of bacon or three.)

153. TEST YOURSELF. If you already exercise (or even if you don't), test your capabilities. If you've always wanted to start an exercise routine, you need to establish a baseline. Consider today a chance to learn about yourself. Use this vacation to set a benchmark for what you'll do in the future. Some examples of things you might measure:

- How many push-ups can you do?
- How many sit-ups can you do in a minute?
- Can you touch your toes? If not, how low can you go?
- How many jumping jacks can you perform in a minute?
- If you run, how long does it take you to complete a mile?

When you return home, choose one of these exercises and keep going. For example, if you did 30 pushups, add one more every day.

154. TRY SOMETHING DIFFERENT. Exercise is a routine many people do consistently at home. But is your routine a little too...routine? Since you're on vacation, consider mixing things up. How? Complete this sentence: "At home, I always ...." Whatever that thing is, do the opposite. You're trying to do things differently, to expose yourself to new ways and new possibilities. So if you always drink coffee, for example, try tea. Or if you always eat meals at a certain time, mix that up. Maybe eat smaller meals more often. Whatever feels different than what you're used to, try that.

155. TAKE THE STAIRS. An easy way to incorporate more exercise in your life is to cut out "time savers" like elevators. If you're in a hotel or on a ship, take the stairs when possible. I'm not suggesting you do it the entire way. If your room is on the eighteenth floor of the hotel, or if you'd have to take eight flights of stairs from your deck to the pool, relax, you don't need to avoid the elevator altogether. But maybe start with a commitment to take just one flight of stairs, then use the elevator. If your journey is ten flights, walk up one, then take the elevator the rest of the way. If you want to push yourself, add more walking flights as the week progresses.

156. TAKE A HIKE. No, I don't mean get lost. I mean take a walk. If you're in a location with natural beauty such as a beach, lake, forest, or desert, go for a long walk – maybe an hour or more. Enjoy your surroundings, especially if the scenery isn't something you typically have at home.

157. KICK OFF YOUR DANCING SHOES. Actually, no, put them on. You know, that phrase makes no sense. You need your dancing shoes to dance, and since you're on vacation, let there be dancing. Have you noticed that in most vacation destinations, it's easy to go dancing? Cruise ships, resorts, and many hotels offer live music and active nightclubs. So, you don't have to drive anywhere. Just go. Recharge with a little electric slide or country line dancing.

YOUR INNER CHILD

158. KICK THE CAN. Whether you're traveling with kids or not, why not have fun acting like a kid? Growing up, you probably played games like kick-the-can or hide-and-go-seek. What if you and several other adults played a game like that now? You might dismiss the idea. "Play kick-the-can? We'd look like fools!" Maybe.

But I recall the classic *Twilight Zone* episode of the same name, where a stick-in-the-mud retiree scorned the playful nature of his rest-home friends who invited him to play outdoors. He tried to get them in trouble for breaking the rules, but going outside, he found his friends had become young again, all because they played kick-the-can. Remember, you're on vacation. You'll probably never see most of these people again. Have some fun. Kick a can or two.

159. BUILD A CASTLE. If you're at the beach, build a sandcastle. Yes, even if you're an adult. Think back to when you were a kid visiting the ocean. Aside from swimming in the waves, the other activity you certainly did was build a sandcastle. The bigger the better. Mine would have moats and swimming pools. Then the tide would come in and wash it away, which was always part of the fun. As adults, we don't build sandcastles. Maybe we should. Much like gardening or knitting, doing things manually with our hands can be relaxing. Start building!

160. RIDE A BIKE. If your destination has bikes available, rent or borrow one and see where it takes you. Just like building sandcastles, this is an activity many of us did as a kid but then abandoned as an adult. If walking isn't your thing, riding a bike is a great way to cover a greater distance and see more sights. Bonus points for getting a deck of playing cards and putting them in the spokes.

161. GO FLY A KITE. Here's another fun activity we did all the time as kids. Ironically, the usual meaning of this phrase is a vaguely hostile way to tell someone to leave you alone. But since you're on vacation, you can turn it around. Make flying a kite fun again. If you're in a destination known for being windy, find a local souvenir spot that has kites for purchase.

162. GET EXHILARATED. Find exciting things to do. As kids, we had a taste for excitement. As adults, we tend to see the risk in everything. As a result, we play it safe and stick to the same-old safe-and-sane

activities. But why not add a little thrill-seeking to your vacation? The safe kind of course. You might zip-line for the first time. Or parasail. Or jump on a banana boat towed by a ski boat. Go surfing or jet-skiing. Learn how to windsurf. Anything out of your comfort zone.

163. READING IS FUNDAMENTAL. Are you a reader? Vacation can be a great time to begin, continue or finish a book. You're reading this book, so well done! You're a reader! And you are reading that has the potential to improve your life. That's not a small thing.

Many people read on vacation, but the things they consume are more escapist in nature. Crime novels, romances, spy thrillers, gossip magazines. There's nothing wrong with these in moderation. It's like eating cotton candy. It tastes good, it's satisfying at the moment. But if you're looking for something substantial, read a book like this one. If you have an e-reader or tablet, check out other books you could download right now.

164. READ SOMETHING UPLIFTING. If you can download a book or buy one in a local book shop, find something of a spiritual or positive nature. This doesn't necessarily have to be religious, though it can be.

Maybe there's an author you want to check out — Deepak Chopra, Gabby Bernstein, Tony Robbins, Joel Osteen, Jon Acuff, Rachel Hollis, Jay Shetty, Michael Singer, the Dalai Lama, Abraham-Hicks — anyone who offers a positive perspective on life. I mentioned in the preface that the origins of this book came from my own experience reading something positive while sitting by the pool in Hawaii. Any reading you do that expands your view of life is a good thing.

165. SHARING IS FUNDAMENTAL. If you are reading a new book this week, and you find interesting thoughts, share them with family or friends. Any time you have to summarize a passage you've read, it helps cement that knowledge in your mind.

4

NURTURE STRONGER RELATIONSHIPS

62 Ways to Connect More Deeply

Is someone sitting in the chair next to you? Unless you're traveling solo, you are likely vacationing with someone you know, someone with whom you're in a relationship. A family member, a spouse, a parent, or a friend.

Without looking at them — *I said don't look!* — get a picture in your mind of what your relationship is like with that person. Back home, before you left for vacation, you had a particular relationship with each person in your life. You communicated a certain way with them. You had certain expectations of each other. And you probably had familiar patterns and routines of how you interacted with others. But now you're on vacation. So, what's that relationship going to be like? Will it be the same? Or could it be...different?

Often when we travel, we take ourselves on the trip. That sounds absurd, doesn't it? If I go on a vacation, of course, I'm the one going. I can't go without me. *Duh!* So yes, that's true in a physical sense. If you go somewhere, *you* go somewhere. But which version of you goes?

By default, most of us take the "home" version of ourselves when we travel. Whoever I was at home, that's who I am on vacation. Whatever habits and patterns and ways of doing things I have at home, I take those on vacation. The way I behaved toward others, the way I engaged in relationships — that's likely the same way I act when I go on vacation. It happens by default.

I suggest you consider an alternative. What if — and I know this may sound slightly radical — but what if you could be a slightly different person on vacation than you are at home? What would that look like?

- You could discover new things about yourself and others
- You could deepen relationships
- You could try new or different things
- You could become someone different

Right about now, you might be thinking this sounds like a lot of work. After all, you just want to relax in your recliner and drink your piña colada. Read your mystery book. And hey, I'm with you. *Most of the time.* I like my piña coladas just as much as the next person.

But if you're on vacation, why not consider it a real vacation. Why not take a vacation from the way you engage in your relationships? At home, there's the version of you that interacts with people in a certain way. Why can't there be a "vacation version" of you?

Again, you might think, "Can't I just relax without thinking about who I am, and without having to talk to people all the time? Can't I just save that for when I get home?" Well, you can. But will you? Really?

For most of us, when we're at home, we don't have time to just hang out. We're too busy. We rush from one thing to another. We have packed schedules. We're going in all directions, 18 hours a day. And everyone else in our life is going in the opposite direction. Sometimes they overlap. When they do, we might call this "dinner." As in, my schedule and yours overlapped in the evening, when both of us needed to eat, so let's have dinner. Yay! What a victory in our relationship! So yes, if you think you're more likely to deepen your relationships when you get home, think again.

When you're on vacation, you can live your life however you want. You have as much time as you want. Well, maybe you don't have unlimited time. If your vacation is one week long, you have one week. But however much time you have, consider it a perfect opportunity to deepen the connections you have with your fellow travelers. (And if you're traveling solo, consider deepening the "connection" you have with yourself.)

In this chapter, I encourage you to think about the relationships you're in and be open to some creative ways you can deepen those bonds.

If you're traveling with multiple people — like a spouse and your kids, or friends and a parent — you might choose to focus on just one key relationship this week. Whichever relationship you choose to focus on, challenge yourself to open up to those people. Learn from them, have fun with this experience, and try new things. Who knows? You may return home a new person.

LET'S START WITH YOU

166. FIRST THERE'S YOU. Let's learn more about the person who should be your favorite person in the whole world: you. In the book and movie *Bridget Jones's Diary*, the title character created lists about herself. Things she liked. Things she didn't. Habits. Opinions. Frustrations. Dreams. Have you ever done that? It can be fun. Take some time today to make lists about yourself, as it relates to travel and vacation. You might make a list then rank the items. Think of the list as "These are a few of my favorite things." Your list might include:

- What types of vacations have you taken before? (e.g., cruise, beach, ski, cultural, adventure, road trip, camping)
- Where have you previously vacationed?
- How would you rank the destinations?
- What are your favorite types of places to visit?
- What museums or cultural destinations have you been to?
- How many "Seven Wonders" or UNESCO sites have you seen?
- How many destinations have you visited?
- How many airports have you flown through?
- What hotels have you stayed in? Which ones stand out?
- Where would you still like to visit?
- What experiences are on your bucket list?

167. NOW ASK WHY. Lists are fun, but they can be superficial. (I think this is a lesson Bridget Jones learned.) They cover the surface-level

version of you. But deep down, who are you? Take one or two of the things from above, and add a twist. Ask yourself "why."

For example, look at the types of vacations you tend to take, then ask "why." If you like beach vacations, why is that? Take a few minutes to come up with your "because." Something like, "I enjoy beach vacations because I love swimming in warm water, I love the sensation of sand between my toes, and I love watching the sunset on the ocean horizon." Did you know that about yourself? Now you do!

This might be especially helpful in planning your next travel experience. Once you know why you like certain experiences, you can plan more of them. Or — radical notion here — you might challenge yourself to move out of your comfort zone. If you decide you only like beach vacations in the Caribbean, maybe your next trip could be a beach vacation in a new place, like Spain, France, or Thailand.

168. AREAS TO IMPROVE? Staying on the subject of you, let's make a personal ledger sheet. Here's how: on a piece of paper, make a line down the middle of the page. On the left, list 2–3 things you're good at. On the right, brainstorm 2–3 areas where you can improve.

For instance, you might write down you are an excellent speaker, that you're good at swimming, and that you're good at chess. That goes on the left. On the right side, you might know you have trouble focusing and seeing things to completion. Or maybe you know you're impatient. Whatever you think of, either good or bad, write down three things you're good at, and three things where you can improve.

169. GO DEEPER. Once you create your ledger sheet, dig deeper. Explore each item. As you think about it, ask yourself "why." Why are you good at certain things, and why are you weak in other areas? If you know you're an impatient person, ask why. Do you want to be that way? Is there some benefit to it? If not, you might consider working on this tendency. Or if you're good at something, and you know why, maybe that will cause you to double down on that quality and add even more of that aspect to your life.

170. THE STORY OF ME. Many people read biographies on vacation. It's a fun way to feel you're part of someone else's life for a short time. You learn about them, why they made the choices they did, and how they become the person they were. But as you're holding that book in

your hands, can you imagine what it would be like if those pages told the story of *your* life? What if you wrote your biography?

Now, I'm not suggesting you write an entire book on vacation. That would take longer than one week. However, you could write a few short paragraphs about yourself that would be something you could share with people in the future.

You could start with a list of pertinent chronological details about your life. From there, you could get creative. If you have a hobby or interest, weave that into the details of your life. Challenge yourself to start small. Don't overthink it. You can add to it when you get home. Hint: make it easier on yourself and dictate your thoughts using your smartphone. You can edit it later.

171. KIDS AUTOBIOGRAPHY. Ask your kids to write their autobiography. It can be fascinating to see what they think of their life so far. We know the moments and events we might write about. But have you ever heard them share their perspective on who they are? If they're not sure where to begin, ask them what they think are their biggest accomplishments, the things they're most proud of, the people they like the most, and the memories that stand out.

172. MY LIFE FROM NOW ON. If you want to have fun with the biography, write a pretend biography that would describe the life you could lead from this point forward. For example, imagine it's twenty years from now. Between now and then, you could do anything you want in your life. You could achieve anything. From that future viewpoint, imagine all the events and accomplishments in your life up until that moment. Now, write a short biography (again, maybe a few paragraphs) about who you intend to become. What kinds of things would you write about? What additional things might you do that you aren't currently doing?

173. JUST A TYPICAL DAY. Another approach for writing your future biography is to imagine your perfect life, and picture what an average day would be like. Pick any day in your intended biography and write about it. For instance, write about the day you started that new business, finished that marathon, or moved into your new house. What do those days feel like? Yes, these things haven't happened yet. But if you write about them as if they have, it creates positive energy that can turn the dream into a reality.

174. WHEN I GROW UP... Ask your children to try this game, especially if they've already expressed what they imagine their future life will be like.

Suggest they pick a typical day when they're an adult, say around age 30, and have them describe what they'll do, who they'll work with, and what they'll accomplish. If they've previously said, "I want to be a doctor," or "I want to design buildings," ask them what a day would look like for someone who does that. Take notes, as it will be fun to share this with them later in life (especially if end up in that job!)

175. TO DREAM THE IMPOSSIBLE DREAM. You have your current life path, and that's fine. But what if you were someone completely different? Who would you choose to be? You might imagine a more realistic version of your potential life, as we did above. Alternatively, you could get slightly crazy with this. Write a completely silly version of your life.

For instance, if you've ever imagined being a professional athlete, write a pretend biography about your career, who you played against, and all your accomplishments. How many NFL rings do you have? What were your greatest accomplishments? Does your home arena fly a banner from the rafters honoring your legendary status? *Yes, I said it was silly, didn't I?* But you're on vacation, why not have fun? Other possible "silly" biography ideas: the day I won the Oscar; the week I climbed that mountain; my dinner with the Dalai Lama.

176. KIDS DREAM THE DARNEDEST THINGS. In #174, you asked your kids what they currently imagine their life will be like around age 30. Now ask them to shoot for the moon. Tell them whatever life they previously shared is valid. But ask them, is there something even bigger they could imagine? Kids usually have no trouble imagining themselves doing incredible things. Ask them to write a short story about who they dream of becoming.

WHO IS YOUR SPECIAL SOMEONE?

177. GETTING TO KNOW YOU. If you're traveling with a spouse, boyfriend, or girlfriend, let's talk about them now. Since you're on a trip together, you may feel you know them well. You don't travel with strangers, right? (Author's note to himself: Idea for next book?) So yes, you're traveling with a non-stranger. You know enough about them to

have decided to travel together. But when it comes to travel, there's a lot we don't know about people, even if we've been in a relationship with them for years.

A fun game to play with your traveling companion is to ask questions like these:

- Where else have you vacationed?
- What is the furthest place to which you've traveled?
- What's the longest vacation you've taken?
- What is the hottest place you've been? The coldest?
- What's your favorite place and why?
- What's the most luxurious travel experience you've ever had?
- What are the most "roughing it" experience you've ever had?
- What's the most exhilarating thing you've done on vacation?
- What's the most scared or worried you've been while traveling?

178. WHERE TO NEXT? Ask your traveling companion this question: if time and money were no object, where would they go next on vacation? What would they do? How long would they stay? What's interesting about this question is that it's easy for us to assume we can't do something. We add it to the "I can't do that" ledger. We think it will cost too much or take too much time. But what if it didn't? What if that travel experience you longed for was more attainable than you imagined? Playing this game is a fun way to explore what's possible in life. Yes, that travel experience might *currently* be out of reach. But if it's a dream, maybe you could make a long-term plan to realize it. It might not be this year or next. But maybe in five years. Who knows? (You do!)

179. LET'S MOVE HERE! Whenever I visit a place for the first time, if I fall in love with the destination, I find myself daydreaming about moving there. In this fantasy, I imagine selling everything and buying some local business so that I can live the (supposed) good life. I can't tell you how many Caribbean bars I have imaginarily bought. Do you feel that way about your current destination? If so, ask your spouse if you'd ever consider living here.

Daydream about what it would be like to live here. What would you do for a living? If you're already retired, how would you spend your days? Who knows, you might find your spouse has had the same fantasies you have. This could be the start of something big.

180. IT'S YOURS! Let's say you have a checkbook with one "unlimited" check in it. If you're saying, "What's a checkbook?" then imagine you have one swipe on a platinum card with no limit. And this week you get to buy one thing. No matter the cost, it's yours.

Now, what would you buy? You might know right away. Or you might want to take your time "shopping." As you travel around all week, consider one thing you might buy with your check. If you make a choice, great! If you find something later in the week you'd rather have, just "trade-in" your existing choice for the new one.

The only rule I'd suggest is rather than being practical, have fun with your choice. Don't say, "I'd buy that 900-room hotel because it would yield 6% EBFTD cash flow." That's smart, it's practical. But I'm looking for fun, something that makes you come alive. For example, you might see a cool beachfront bar with lots of character and decide to buy that because you could see yourself watching the sunset while shaking up mai tais and engaging in fun conversations. Once you've done this yourself, pose the question to your spouse, family, or friend.

181. "HELLO, I'M...." Here's something to do with your spouse or significant other. Pretend to meet each other for the first time. Arrange to find one another at a bar before dinner, and act as if you know nothing about each other. A classic example of this game comes from the TV show *Modern Family*, where the two adult parents, Phil and Claire, pretend they don't know each other. On Valentine's Day, they meet at a bar. They play-act as characters different from their usual personas. They engage in playful banter, which hopefully leads to an amorous evening. You might not go this far, but some variation of this could be a fun way to get to know each other.

182. THE INTERVIEW. You could also treat this "first-time" meeting not as a romantic encounter, but as a journalist interview. One of you could pretend to be a journalist, and the other the subject of a biography interview. The fun in the game is to try to put aside everything you know about the "subject," and ask unexpected questions which elicit new and interesting information.

183. IF YOU COULD STAY ANYWHERE... Here's a fun question to pose to your traveling companion. Imagine this scenario: you could AirBNB any house in the world for one week. Now pretend it's a famous person's home. Whose would you choose? George Clooney's

place in Italy? Bill Gates' lakefront home in Seattle? Richard Branson's island in the Caribbean? Or maybe a ski chalet in Aspen, or a beachfront house in Maui? For each choice, ask the person why they picked that location, and how they'd spend their time.

FAMILY

First, a preface for this section. Whether you're traveling as a couple or with children, the next activities can strengthen your relationships. Many of these can be done over a leisurely breakfast or dinner.

So pick one meal and spend an hour focused on each other. Why do this? To learn more about each other. If you make a conscious decision to learn something about each person, you'll become a better listener on this trip.

Yes, 60 minutes may seem like forever to those of us who have hectic schedules at home, whereas 20 minutes at the dinner table can seem like an eternity. But there are lots of ways to fill this time and enjoy the experience. In any case, you're on vacation. You should have more time with each other. Take advantage of it!

184. HOW WAS YOUR DAY? Over a meal, ask everyone to share their favorite experience of the day. Ask them to describe it briefly, how it made them feel, and why they chose that moment. The experience they share doesn't have to be a huge life-changing event, though it might be. If you went sky diving that day, then yes, it's likely you would say that was your favorite experience of the day. But the answer could also be something simple. Maybe it was a meaningful interaction with someone. The way the sun reflected on the ocean. A song they heard. An insight gained. Or an accomplishment like having the first-ever conversation in another language.

185. WRITE IT DOWN. Write down everyone's answers in your vacation journal. Be sure to note why they chose this experience. Imagine if they said their favorite moment was a thoughtful clerk who helped them, and the moment stood out because "That person cared about me." This kind of answer could give you insights as to what each family member values and wants to experience.

186. COMPARED TO HOME. Discuss something you learned about your destination or the place you are staying. Pay attention to how it differs from home. Sometimes we visit a place and we're surprised

at the ways they're both similar and different. I recall visiting the Caribbean island of St. Martin and learning that families build their homes over long periods. Mortgages are uncommon there, so they add sections and even stories to their home as they have the money. They had homes but they built and financed them differently.

Kind of interesting, right? Questions to ponder about your destination:

- What is the same here as at home? What is different?
- How are towns and cities laid out?
- What are the most common business or stores?
- How do people get around?
- What does this place have that you don't have at home?
- Are there similarities that surprise you?
- Who have you met today that was interesting?

187. IF YOU LIVED HERE… Ask everyone to share what they imagine a day in their life would be like if they lived here. What would they do? If they had a job, what would it be? If they're in school, what do they imagine they would study? Would you even want to live here?

188. THAT PERSON IS…INTERESTING. Play an improvisation game based on someone or something interesting. For example, let's say you are at dinner, and you see someone across the restaurant that is colorful or unique in some way (or maybe you saw this person earlier in the day.) You might consider making up a story about them and how they got here, or what they are doing. Don't be mean or judgmental, or otherwise make fun of them. Also, try not to stare. Just use your imagination and spin a fun little story about them.

189. DISNEY WORLD FOREVER! In #178 above, you asked your traveling companion where they would travel if time and money were no object. This can also be a fun question to pose to kids. Ask where they would go on vacation if they could. We assume the answer would be an obvious choice like Disney World. But you might be surprised by the answers. If they do pick a familiar theme park, broaden the question. Ask what's one country they'd like to visit. This might lead to ideas for future travel.

190. WOULD MOM AND DAD GO WITH YOU? A good follow-up question to #189 is, "Would I be coming with you on this vacation?" Again, it's likely they would say yes. Especially younger kids. But older

kids approaching their independence might tell you, "I think I could do it on my own." If you never ask this question, you might not know how they feel about their level of maturity.

191. YOU GET A CHECK! AND YOU GET A CHECK! (I've been waiting for this Oprah gag the whole book. Thanks for indulging me.)

Like #180 above, give each family member a blank check they can use to buy anything they see the whole week. At the end of each day, ask what they would have bought. If you do this as a family, consider letting the kids go first so they aren't influenced by what their parents choose. Parents are more likely to choose dream businesses like a scuba shack, Parisian café, or Caribbean bar. But you might be surprised what your kids choose. Once they make a choice, let them change their mind from day to day, if they find something they like better. Perhaps set a deadline, toward the end of the week, where everyone's choice is final. And no, their choice doesn't have to fit in the overhead bin on the flight.

192. TELL ME MORE... If you're traveling with an extended family, such as grandparents or aunts and uncles, take this opportunity to learn more about them. It's easy to assume we know everything about the people in our lives until someone asks us a question that stumps us. Questions like, where did your parents go to school? Or, how long did you live in a certain place? Hearing these, we realize we don't know as much as we thought. Use your week together to learn more about your family's history. To keep the conversation flowing, use phrases like, "Tell me more," "What was that like?" "How did you feel about that?" or "Was that common then?"

193. 23 AND YOU. Create a family tree. Take a piece of paper to your meal and ask grandparents to fill in the branches on their family tree. You could start by asking your kids if they know who is in their family tree. This kind of activity can be fun as a prompt to solicit stories nobody's ever heard.

194. WHEN I WAS YOUR AGE... Speaking of extended family you're traveling with, ask them questions about *their* vacation history. I'm always surprised when I talk to people my parents' age and discover, for example, that their honeymoon was three days long and they stayed in rather modest accommodations. It certainly puts things in

perspective compared to how most of us travel these days. Questions to ask could include:

- What places have they visited?
- What's their favorite travel experience?
- When did they take their first vacation?
- How often did they travel? More than once a year?
- What was their honeymoon like?
- What airline did they typically fly?
- What was it like to fly in their day? Did they dress up?
- What's the longest vacation they've ever taken?
- Have they been to a country that no longer exists?
- Did they put those travel stickers on their luggage?
- Do they still have postcards or pictures from their travels?

By the way, this can be a great conversation to have around your kids, who may not realize that previous generations weren't as well-traveled as their own.

DO THINGS TOGETHER

You might be thinking the conversation games I've described above could get old after the first couple of evenings together. What does "old" look like? You might break out the "How was your day?" hoping for genuinely interesting replies. Instead, you get a sullen "Fine."

For example, you: "What did you do?" Them: "Nothing." You: "What was your favorite activity?" Them: "Sleeping." Okay, yes it does sound like a parent's dialogue with their teenager.

If your conversations on vacation sound like this, consider changing up the activities during which you have the discussions. Most of us are familiar with the dynamic of a conversation around the dinner table. Like a French baguette, it can get stale. By changing what you're physically doing, you may stimulate pathways to deeper conversations.

195. GO ON A DATE. If you're traveling as a family, have a "date" or special experience with each family member. If you're a dad, and you have two kids, do something special with each one. Schedule it in advance. Pick an activity each child will like. Maybe a special lunch,

a hike, visiting a museum, going on their favorite theme park ride, or anything that will be special to each of you.

196. GO ON A PICNIC. Whether it's you, your spouse, or your whole family, grab some food and go on a picnic. This could be lunch or early evening supper. Where will you get the food? If a local market or convenience store offers picnic fare, buy from there. If your hotel offers take-out options, that works too.

If it's a group or family experience, let each person pick one favorite food item to share. No blanket? No problem. Borrow a beach towel or ask your hotel for a table cloth. If you plan to buy a souvenir beach towel, use it for your picnic. Changing up your environment from the dinner table to sitting under a tree hopefully changes the dynamics of how you relate to your travel companions.

197. PLAY GAMES. Kids love playing games, but somehow as adults, we forget the joys of summer favorites like kick-the-can or I-spy. If you're traveling with kids, ask them if there's a game they'd like to play. Have a paper airplane contest (furthest flight wins.) Hold a pool regatta with paper boats, blowing into the "sails" to reach a finish line.

198. GO FLY A KITE. If your travel destination has kites for sale — especially at a beach destination — this is a must-do. Kids love kites, but again, who says a grown-up couple can't have fun building and sailing a kite in the sky?

199. TOUR DE VACATION. Vacation bike rides are the best, especially if they're easy to rent and in a convenient location. The best kind of location for bike riding would be a beach boardwalk with no vehicular traffic to worry about. The not-so-best location would perhaps be New York City. If you're not sure where to find bikes, ask your hotel or do an internet search for your location and "bike rental." Of course, wear a helmet and follow safety laws.

200. BACK TO SCHOOL. Take a lesson in something such as lei making, painting, or sculpture. If there's a sport you've always wanted to try like tennis, sailing, windsurfing, or stand-up paddleboarding, sign up for a class in that. If possible, find an activity everyone in your group might enjoy.

201. GAME NIGHT! Pick a board game (hotels and ships often have these) and play together as a group. Playing Monopoly at home is one

thing. But zooming past Go! and collecting $200, all while watching the sunset... it's a whole different game.

202. GET COOKING! If you happen to be staying in a condo and you're making some of your meals, involve your group or family in preparing one (or more!) meals. Make a production of it and create teams where everyone plays a role. Someone can research recipes online. Decide on the final menu as a group.

Go shopping together for the ingredients (if there's a farmers market, shop there.) On the day of the meal, everyone contributes a skill in food preparation. Cutting, washing, stirring, setting the table, filling water glasses – there's a job for everyone. And working as a team will make you closer as a family.

203. YOU DECIDE! Do one excursion or outing the kids choose. Come up with a list of 3–5 activities, then let them decide. Of course, they should be things that fit your schedule and budget. The beauty of this is that even if they choose the one activity you would've chosen anyway, they now feel it was their choice. Give them a sense of ownership. This is their vacation too. If you have a variety of ages, try to choose one they all agree on.

204. READING IS FUN-DAMENTAL. Whether you're a couple on vacation or an entire family, pick a book you all might like, and take turns reading aloud. Pick a classic, old, or new, and share the experience of enjoying the story together.

PEOPLE HELPING PEOPLE

205. "MY NAME IS .... AND I'LL BE YOUR CUSTOMER TONIGHT." Get to know more about the people helping you on vacation. If it seems comfortable to do so, engage them in a friendly conversation about their own life. Start simple. If you're sitting at a bar — big shock, that can sometimes happen on vacation — ask the bartender what's their favorite drink. Build from there. If you're in a restaurant, ask the server what's their favorite dish. Follow up. *Why* is that their favorite drink? Or if it's a particular food, *why* do they like that?

You might think it would be difficult to engage a total stranger in conversation. Your task will be made somewhat easier by the fact that the workers you meet on vacation will likely be used to talking to strangers all day long. And it's their job. So relax. It won't be as difficult as you may think.

206. SAY "CHEESE." As you ease into the conversation, ask them where to find the best picture opportunities. They probably see guests snapping photos all the time, so they would know, right? Consider them an expert. Ask where the best locations are. Where are the hidden spots? Is there a particular time of day that's ideal for picture taking? Where is the best lighting? How can you avoid taking a bad picture in this place? Be sure to thank them for their advice.

207. WHAT'S IT LIKE TO LIVE HERE? Assuming this is their home (or at least their work home) ask them about it. Think of this person as an expert on your vacation destination. They spend every day here. They are probably a wealth of information. Tap into it. Ask them what the must-see attraction is, and if they would recommend it. If so, ask them the best time to visit, and if they have any other recommendations. If you're not currently near their home (e.g., on a cruise ship), they could still tell you about some destination or attraction where they're from.

208. WHERE DO LOCALS HANG OUT? When you ask what's a must-see attraction, be prepared for them to give you the standard tourist response. "Oh, you have to see this museum, bridge, statue, or photo spot." And tourist spots are fine. But you might also ask them to share something only locals know about (or people who ask locals!) Some examples might be, "Where's the best place to get fresh fruit?" "Where do local people shop?" "What's a good (non-touristy) place for each lunch?" "Where do YOU buy your food?" "Is there a beach (or park) where locals go?"

209. LOCAL CUSTOMS. Delve deeper in your exploration. Go beyond the expected. Ask them what they love about their home. Not the sightseeing attractions, the beach, the cafes, or the museums. Rather, ask about the people, their neighbors. Maybe they'll share a local greeting. Or a piece of wisdom that's passed down through families. Or even funny superstitions. Ask them, "What's one thing that people here *never* do, and what's one thing they *always* do?"

210. TELL ME MORE... Having explored their thoughts about the destination, if you feel the conversation is going well, next ask them

more about themselves. An easy starting point is to ask about their job. Use questions like:

- How did they get this job?
- How long have they been doing it?
- What's an average workweek like?
- What did they do before they had this particular job?
- What do people find surprising about their job?
- If they could do any other job, what would it be?
- Where do they see their career going?

The insights you gain from this are especially valuable to share with children, to broaden their perspective on the world.

Kids don't often realize how hard other people in the world work. Mom and Dad get the weekend off, so it's easy to assume that's how it is for everyone. Conversations like this can make kids more aware of how other people live and work.

211. HOW DO YOU SAY... If you're in a destination where another language is spoken, ask your new friend how to say a few words or phrases in their language. You might start with obvious useful ones, like "please" and "thank you." During your vacation, try out your new foreign vocabulary. By the way, "thank you" will be super helpful at the end of your conversation, right?

212. WHERE DO *YOU* VACATION? As you establish a deeper rapport in your conversation, ask more personal questions. Have they always lived in this location? Where do they like to travel when they have time off? How much vacation time do they get? What places have they visited? What's a typical day-off look like? What do they do in their free time? What's on their bucket list of places to visit? Ask them to elaborate on their answers. Follow up with "Why..." As in, "Why do you want to go there?"

213. HAVE YOU EVER HEARD OF... While you're talking about their home, be willing to talk about where you're from. Ask them what they know about your home. If they haven't heard of your specific town, broaden the question to the nearest city, state, province, or country. What have they heard about it? You might tell them about a must-see attraction, in case they ever visit your neck of the woods.

214. LET'S SAY I GAVE YOU A HUUUUGE TIP... Along the lines of #180 and #191 above, ask the person you're talking to, what's one thing they would buy if they had a blank check. A new business? A home addition? School for a child? Money to help parents? Travel? Compare their answers to your own.

STRANGERS (AKA, POTENTIAL FRIENDS)

215. MAKE NEW FRIENDS. It's also fun to talk with new people when you're traveling. Who knows, maybe you'll chat up other tourists. Or maybe you'll have a conversation with a local.

Now I can imagine what you're thinking. "I don't like talking with people I've never met." That's not uncommon. Most of us can find it challenging to speak with new people.

The most likely reason why is we're afraid of being judged by that person. What if we attempt a conversation with someone, and they ignore us? Or they don't want to talk? Or they ridicule us? Or they hear our innocuous conversation starter as something like, "Can I rub suntan lotion on you?" Each of these scenarios is possible, except maybe the last one, and while they might be true, are they *probable*? Likely not. So put aside the worst-case scenarios for a moment.

You could just as easily imagine, what if my conversation goes well and I make a new friend? What if I meet my new *best* friend? How awesome would that be? Pretty awesome! So, between these two extremes — potential ridicule and lifelong besties — there's a good possibility you'll be able to carry out a brief conversation with someone you've just met. Still skeptical? Just get started.

Here are some icebreaker questions you can use to strike up a conversation with people you don't know (yet):

- Do you like that book? (assuming they're reading a book.)

Okay, see that wasn't hard. Let's keep going...

- How long have you been here?
- How long did it take you to get here?
- How was your flight?

See, this is easy. You can do this!

- Is this the first time you've been here?
- (If not...) Does it live up to your expectations?
- What's your favorite part of the destination?
- What's your favorite restaurant here?
- What's your favorite thing you've done so far?
- What would you recommend seeing or doing while here?
- Any mistakes you've made, or things you'd avoid?
- What has surprised you?
- (If in a foreign country) Did you learn any language phrases?
- What other people have you met?
- Any great employees you've met?
- What other places do you like to visit?

See, that wasn't so bad, was it? You're a natural at this!

216. THE 5 SECOND RULE. *What's that, you still haven't tried talking to a new person yet?* I think I know why. The moment you consider walking over to that total stranger, your mind comes up with all the reasons why it's a terrible idea (I listed many of those in #215 above.) Best-selling author Mel Robbins has a solution for you: her "5 Second Rule," from her book of the same name. Here's how it works:

The moment you get the idea to do something — strike up a conversation with someone new, for example — you start a countdown from 5 to 1, and then you do the very thing. So, 5...4...3...2...1... action! This process prevents your brain from telling you why you shouldn't do that thing and gets you to take action. So, if you can think of lots of reasons not to start up a conversation with someone you don't know, use the 5 Second Rule and just do it.

217. ONE NEW FRIEND A DAY. Now that you can chat with strangers with a snap of your fingers, why not set a goal to meet one new person a day while on vacation? I'm not suggesting you need to advance a conversation to the point where you press for their email or Instagram. You might not get their name at all. Don't put the pressure of an outcome on the conversation. Just decide you'll have one conversation a day with someone new. Write about it in your vacation journal. "Chatted with someone by the pool today. They just flew in from .... They ate at the sushi place last night and liked it." See? Simple!

218. OTHER PARENTS. If you're traveling with kids, and you happen to speak to other parents, ask them what they've learned from their kids so far. How will you know if they have kids? Oh, that will probably be obvious. They'll be the ones with the least amount of time for themselves, or possibly the biggest empty mai tai glass collection. Here are some questions you could start with:

- How are their kids liking the trip so far?
- How was their flight? (Assuming you flew here.)
- Are they adapting okay to the (hotel/ship) room?
- What are their favorite activities so far?
- What are their favorite foods?
- What do they wish there was more of?
- What do they not like?
- What rides or attractions did they love?
- Would they want to come back here again (if not, why?)
- Where would they rather go instead?
- What unexpected things did their kids say or do?
- What have they done more than once?

If the conversation goes deeper, you can get more philosophical...

- Has anything surprised them about their kids?
- What challenges have they faced?
- What made their kids smile or laugh the most?
- What other destinations have their children loved?
- What will the kids miss the most?
- What were they reluctant to do, but then enjoyed?
- What have the parents learned about their kids on this trip?

219. JOIN ME IN A SELFIE. If you do happen to befriend another tourist or even a local, take a picture with your new acquaintance. If you think they are hesitant, or maybe reluctant to take a picture with you — them: "What if they share this picture on Facebook with the caption, 'Lame person I met by the pool'?" — you could preface the request by saying the picture's just for your vacation album — not on social — so that you can remember the interesting people you spoke with. If they don't seem concerned by your request or suggest you're free to post the selfie online, consider it an opportunity to caption the photo with, "A fun new person I met on vacation."

220. WANT ME TO TAKE YOUR PICTURE? Speaking of pictures, if you see the opportunity, offer to take somebody else's picture. You can generally tell when people — say a couple — are trying to figure out how they're going to take the ideal selfie. We've all been there. Whenever I see this situation, I ask if they would like me to take it for them. Rarely does someone decline. It's funny. People are willing to hand their $800 smartphone to a total stranger. I think this speaks to the general trust we want to place in others and our openness to meeting new friends.

221. CARE TO JOIN US? Ask people if they would like to join you for a drink, a game, or some other activity that might be fun doing together. Maybe these might be the new friends you met while taking their pictures. Whoever it is, consider spending some relaxed time with the people you just met. Though do avoid a misleading vibe that says, "We saw you from across the room and dig your style."

222. A TABLE FOR EIGHT? Look for opportunities to share a meal with new friends. This may seem risky. Spending an hour with people I've barely met? That's crazy! Maybe. But some of my favorite vacation experiences have been sharing a meal with people I'd just met.

My first vacation as an adult was at a Club Med in Mexico. At the time, you sat for dinner at tables with eight guests. If you entered as a solo traveler, like I was, the hostess would seat you with others. This was one of the highlights of my Club Med stays — the opportunity to have conversations with people from all over the world.

You may not be in a situation where there's a hostess to seat you, and perhaps it seems forward to ask someone to join you for a drink or meal. That's fine. Don't push this kind of opportunity. If the situation feels comfortable, you'll know.

This can also work well on a cruise. You could roll the dice and ask to be seated at a larger table. If you end up with interesting people the first night, great. If not, ask to be seated elsewhere after that.

223. THIS IS WHERE WE'RE FROM. If you've brought postcards from home, (hint, hint) show these to the people you meet. This can be a good way to share what's unique about where you're from. If you keep a vacation journal with pictures of places you've been, you might also share that.

224. SHARE PHOTOS. If your town doesn't have postcards, create your own. If you read this before you travel, you can print 10–20 pictures of your hometown. You can also quickly create a photo album on your smartphone with pictures to share.

Either way — actual pictures or a smartphone album — if the opportunity comes up to talk about your home, you'll be ready for the show and tell.

If you're reading this before you travel, great! You can create original photos specifically for this purpose. What might you include? Here's a possible "shot list" of pictures to take:

- Your house
- Your kitchen (people love seeing other kitchens)
- Your pets
- Your yard or neighborhood
- Your car
- Your workplace or office
- Your favorite restaurant
- Your favorite clothing store
- Your favorite grocery store
- The meat or vegetable section where you shop
- A civic landmark in your town (statue, building, street, etc.)
- The oldest building in town
- The largest building in town
- Friends and coworkers
- A pretty view or location in your town
- A place you volunteer (church, charity, shelter, etc.)
- An activity or sport you're involved with
- Activities your kids are involved with (sports, music, etc.)
- Something you do every day (Starbucks, walking, shopping)

Sharing pictures like these can result in easy conversation. Showing a picture of your knitting hobby, for example, could prompt that person to share a picture of their hobby. Or a picture of the oldest building in your town might prompt a Londoner to say, "The pub we're sitting in dates to the 1600s." It may also be interesting to discuss what we have in common — like homes, stores, and schools — and what's different. ("Your grocery store looks like that? Wow!")

225. KIDS PHOTO ALBUM. Create a photo album on your smartphone that tells the "story" of your kids' lives. Involve them in the creation. Photos can include their school, activities, favorite toys, friends, hobbies, interests, and favorite things about their town.

If you choose to take these pictures in advance, this could be a fun opportunity to learn more about your child. Imagine asking them a question, "What's your favorite place in town?" and then going to take a picture of it. You'll learn things about them you otherwise might not have known. With this album created in advance, you can easily share images of your family's home life.

226. BE OUR GUEST. If you belong to a service group like Rotary, Kiwanis, or Optimists, see if your group has a meeting in this vacation destination. If so, plan a visit. Attending a meeting on vacation can expose you to new customs and people. Consider exchanging something with a local group. You could bring a token from your group and swap it for something from them.

227. GET SPIRITUAL. Attend a church, synagogue, or spiritual service at your destination. This may not be everyone's preference on vacation, but again it can be interesting to see the differences in how religious services are observed away from home. This practice can be especially meaningful if you're in a destination rich with history.

For example, if I'm in Florence, Italy, I might decide to attend Mass on Sunday morning. I'm not Catholic, and I don't understand Italian, but I can certainly appreciate the beauty and symbolism of a service conducted in a church over 600 years old.

5

CREATE LIFETIME MEMORIES

62 Ways to Bring Back More Than Just Souvenirs

Here's a typical way most of us document what we did on our vacation. We take some pictures or videos. We post them on Facebook or Instagram. If we're fancy, we create a funny caption or overlay on the picture. "There!" we say, "that proves I was at the destination." Pictures taken, vacation done, we find ourselves at the airport for the flight home. And then we remember — *Oh crap! I need to bring back something to give to a friend, co-worker, or relative.*

We dart into an airport souvenir shop and quickly grab something, anything, that will show the recipient how much we care about them, and how much thought we put into it. Does this sound familiar? This is how most of us create memories of the vacation we took.

We have a superficial connection to the experience itself. Yes, we took a picture or bought an item. But what becomes of those? The photos will be lost in our phone's library and the souvenir we bought may end up as a Goodwill donation.

This might not describe you. But if you identify even a little bit, read on. With a little advance thought, the memories you take home can be more meaningful and long-lasting. But why is this important? The more we thoughtfully engage with our vacation, the more likely we are to appreciate the experience.

This is not to say we shouldn't take pictures on vacation. Of course you are going to walk around on holiday with your phone, snapping shots as you go. But we all recognize that with this approach, we aren't engaged with the place we're visiting.

All we are doing is viewing it through the lens of our camera or smartphone. You'll return home with 200–300 random pictures, but you won't have any sense of having been to that place.

Maybe you do more than just snapshots of the actual destination. Maybe you take a selfie, with something memorable in the background. "Look, that's me in front of Trevi Fountain in Rome!" But even with this approach, there's nothing of us at the authentic moment. Because we have no connection to the setting of the place.

The question to ask is, what were you doing at the Trevi Fountain? This is one of the problems of social media. It's trained us to think of photos as a way to say to people on Instagram, "Look where I am! Isn't this amazing!" People comment on the photo or like it, and somehow that makes us feel better.

But is it truly meaningful? I argue not.

The first step to engaging with your vacation is to pause first and think about what you are seeing or experiencing. Notice things about the location. What's the temperature? If there are people in the picture, what are they doing? Take in the details of what you're seeing. Once you've given it some thought, *then* pull out your camera and document what you see. *Notice first, photograph second.*

With this in mind, here are 62 ways you can more authentically engage with the destination, whether it's taking pictures, buying souvenirs, or contributing something of yourself to the destination.

SAY CHEESE!

Most of us will take hundreds, if not thousands, of vacation photos. If you're like me you'll snap pictures of lots of things, assuming you'll sort through them later, curating the ones you like into a sharable format.

But how often does that happen? I find I'm most successful when I pre-organize BEFORE the trip.

When I'm traveling, there are too many things I want to do, places I want to go, naps I want to take, and drinks I want to consume. The key for me is to create photo albums in advance. Then while traveling, I can more easily drop photos into that album.

First, a quick note on terminology. Your smartphone's photos application — and its cloud or computer connection — may have different names for what's considered a folder or album. Your smartphone app may have limited functionality in terms of what you can create on it, vs. what you need to do on your computer. I recommend exploring your specific functionality before you travel so you know in advance what you're going to do.

228. THE JOURNEY OF A THOUSAND PICTURES STARTS WITH ONE ALBUM. Let's make this easy to start. Create one album or folder for this vacation. If you're traveling to Disney World, create a folder into which you can place all your shots. Every picture you take goes there. If you did nothing but this, then yay! You've at least created a home for the hundreds of pictures you'll take.

229. GET ALBUM CRAZY. If you've got additional time, take that one album or folder you created, and add additional albums or folders inside. These would be themed around your specific destination or activity. For example, if you're in Cabo San Lucas, create an album for the beach. Now you can drop all the beach pictures in that album.

The beauty of this system is that the same picture could reside in several albums. A picture of your husband John, on the beach, at sunset, could be placed in three albums: "beach," "sunsets" and "John." Now that you have a sense of this, here are some general category topics you might consider in creating your photo albums:

- Beach
- Sunset
- Family
- Pool
- Ocean
- Food
- Drinks

- Rooms (e.g., your ship or hotel rooms)
- Panorama angles
- Rides
- Characters
- Activities (e.g, swimming, sailing, hiking, climbing)
- Transportation (e.g., ships, airplanes, busses, cars)
- Dining (e.g, cafes, restaurants, unique locations)
- Sports and activities
- Architecture (e.g., buildings, churches, bridges)
- Streets
- Animals
- Location (by day, a city visited, port stop, etc.)
- Specific scenery (e.g., glaciers, mountains, lakes)

You get the idea. Give some advance thought to your vacation, and decide how you would want to categorize your photos. Decide how you'll want to recall your specific pictures. If you're going to France to see the Tour de France, maybe you'll want pictures of each town you visit — that's an album. Maybe you'll ask riders for autographs and selfies. That's an album. You might also take pictures of each spot from which you view the race. Album. You get the idea, right?

230. BEST PICTURES EVER. Create "best of" categories. In addition to all the different thematic album categories, you create and create albums to store your favorites.

I like to create albums with my best 7 pictures, the best 14, the best 21, etc. So on a 7-day trip, each day I decide which is my favorite picture of that particular day and place it in the Best 7 album. My second favorite picture of the day goes into Best 14 (along with the first), my three favorite pictures go the Best 21, etc. This way, if I want to look at my top 7 pictures of the entire trip, they're all in one album. My top 14 pictures are in another. If you keep up with your pictures this way, you'll arrive home with an album ready to share.

231. KID PICTURES. For families with kids who have smartphones or cameras, encourage them to share their favorite picture of the day, and place them in a "Family Favorites Album." For younger kids without a camera, you might occasionally lend your phone or camera to them so they can take pictures of what they like.

232. GET CREATIVE. In addition to the more obvious theme ideas above, take pictures of the unusual or offbeat things you find. For example, if you're visiting a foreign country that has unique billboards, beverage cans, giant lizards, or road signs, document those.

233. MEMORIES. Document first-time experiences with a folder called "First Time." You always remember your first time, especially if you took a picture of it. Many adults may have grown up before smartphone cameras allowed us to document every single moment. But for our kids or companions who have never been to a certain place, consider getting a picture of their reaction.

Visiting the Grand Canyon for the first time is a perfect example. If you have been there before but your traveling partners have not, get a picture the first time they see the Canyon. This would be a fun album to have over your lifetime, a collection of pictures of your face witnessing things for the first time. May as well start now.

234. KIDS TRYING NEW THINGS. Take the above idea and create an album of your kids seeing or trying new things. This could be the first time they saw a new place, tried new food, or experienced a new adventure. You might even use the video feature on your smartphone to ask them what they thought of the experience. If you video the moment, you might ask them the question in a way that sets the context of what they're doing. This will make it easier for you to remember years later what's happening at that moment. For example, you might say on video, "Scott, this is the first time you're trying a kiwi fruit. What do you think?"

235. MY QUIRKY INTERESTS. Along the lines of "First Time" pictures, collect photos with unique things that interest you, not just on this trip, but across all your travel experiences. For example, maybe you are fascinated by unique pool designs. If so, create an album called "pools." Every time you stay somewhere that has a swimming pool, take a creative picture of that pool and drop it in the album. Focus on some aspect of that pool that's unique or interesting. Do this for several years, over numerous trips, and you'll have an album that recalls fun memories of the destination, and captures your interest.

236. FRIENDLY FACES. Take pictures of people who help you. If there are people you meet along the way, ask if they'll take a picture with you. This could be the mixologist at the beach bar, the childcare

person who watched your kids, or the tour guide who led your day-long excursion. Then create an album that spans several trips – maybe call it "Friendly Faces." If you can attach notes to your pictures, you might want to include the person's name and why their service or warmth stood out to you.

237. IT MUST BE A SIGN. Take pictures of intriguing signs, especially if you're traveling in a foreign location with signage different from home. The benefits of this project might not be borne after just one trip. But if you continue with this over the years, on multiple trips, you'll have a fun album of "signs around the world." (Just don't take your pictures while driving, right?)

238. THIS AGAIN? Take pictures of features you are likely to see again and again over the years. For example, what does the beach sand look like in Los Angeles, Mykonos, or the Cayman Islands? By capturing close-up images of things you'll likely see over and over again, you'll create fun photo albums as your vacation experiences expand over the years. Other examples are flowers, trees, and restaurant menus. Be creative!

239. "WOW!" PICTURES. When you're taking pictures, capture moments of intensity. Look for opportunities to do fun, thrilling, exciting things and then take pictures. Maybe it's riding a speed boat, ziplining, jumping off the high dive, surfing or go-carting. Anything in which your subject line is likely to be "WOW!"

240. COLORFUL COCKTAILS. Create an album called "Cocktails" and fill it with the most colorful and interesting drinks you encounter on your trip. Bonus points for asking the bartender the ingredients and mix instructions. Bonus points for seeking out drinks that are specific to this destination, such as the "Bob Marley" in Jamaica.

241. CHEERS TO BEERS! Speaking of drinks, ask a bartender what the most popular local beers are, then take pictures of those. Almost every place has its craft beers. Imagine a photo album with nothing but pictures of local brews.

242. CHRISTMAS (CARD) IN JULY. If you send year-end holiday cards, use your destination as a backdrop for the photo. Often we are in a great mood on vacation. We're relaxed, we smile more, we look happy. This leads to better pictures. Find a backdrop that

reminds you of this location, then take your holiday picture in that setting. If you're on a cruise, or at a resort hotel, they often have an evening where professional photographers are available to take pictures. You're probably dressed nicely for dinner, they have great lighting and photo equipment, so why not take advantage of the opportunity to get a great picture?

243. "AND...ACTION!" Do you take videos on vacation? Just five or ten years ago, you would've had to carry a bulky camcorder on vacation to capture video footage. Now, most of us have smartphones that take extraordinary high-quality video, some even in 4K resolution. As with your pictures, you might place these videos in related albums.

How long should your video be? It depends on your intent. If you know you're going to edit a compilation movie when you get home, having 10–15 seconds of footage for each thing can be helpful. However, if you intend to have a movie to remind you of the experience, film something longer.

For example, I might love the view from the top of a mountain hike. I might film about a minute of the view, holding my camera as still as possible. Once I return home, I can pull up that video and remind myself of the good feeling of the experience.

What types of subjects might you video? Here are some ideas:

New Things. Every time you try something new, like an interesting beverage or unique food, capture yourself on video with the reaction you have to that beverage or food.

Relaxing Things. Film settings you find relaxing. For instance, if you're out on a beach walk in the morning and nobody's around, take a moment to capture 30–40 seconds of the waves rolling in. Perhaps pretty flowers or waterfalls soothe you. Relaxing in a reclining chair, looking at the pool. Whatever experience evokes a feeling of relaxation.

Unique View. If your hotel has a unique vantage — like the Washington Monument — take a video of that. If you're gliding along a canal in Venice, film that. Grand Canyon, the Vatican, a bridge across the Thames in London, a boat ride across the Seine in Paris, or sailing past the Statue of Liberty in New York — those are all iconic experiences you can rewatch again and again.

<u>Walking</u>. Some people can capture good videos walking around. I'm not one of those people. However, if you have a Steadicam or gimble that produces smoother footage, it might be fun to take a few minutes of video walking around your destination.

Of course, be respectful of other people. Don't intrude on their enjoyment of the location. Also, know that some people may not want to be in your video. Early mornings tend to be an ideal time to take this kind of footage. There are fewer people in the shot, so when I re-watch the video, I can focus more on the destination itself.

244. TELL US A STORY. Create a story about your trip, then tell that story through pictures. It could be a chronology of one day. Or a theme. Or a person you met. It might be an experience or challenge you had. It's your story, so be creative! For example, let's say you rent a car for a drive around the island where you're staying. Think about that experience as a story. It has a beginning, middle, and end.

<u>Tell the beginning</u>: here's a picture of John, he helped us rent the car. Here's me opening the sunroof. Here are my backseat passengers buckled in.

<u>Then tell the middle</u>: here are the road signs in another language we didn't understand. Here's the little town we stopped in for a cool drink. Here's the soda bottle. Here are some animals we saw alongside the road. Here's the tree under which we had our picnic.

<u>Then tell the end</u>: here's me filling up the tank at a gas station. Here's the fuel charged in a foreign currency. Here we are standing by the car, safely returned to the lot.

The point is to find interesting observations you can make about the experience, using the lens of your camera. Here's a storytelling tip: look for drama. Look for the challenges in your story and let the pictures tell those challenges.

Have you ever noticed when kids tell a story, they say, "And then... And then... And then..."? This is an example of storytelling that's lacking in drama. Instead of "And then...", think of the moments that are "But..." or "However..."

Returning to the example above, let's say you want to create a video of your picnic. You could take a lovely photo of the blanket under a tree. And that would be nice.

But what if during your picnic, some ants decided to join you, and they got into the food. That's a moment worth a picture. That's a "but…" moment. As in, "We had a lovely picnic under a tree (PICTURE OF TREE), but then some "guests" joined us (PICTURE OF ANTS.)

Do you see how looking for the "But then…" pictures can liven up your vacation photo album? What other kinds of stories might you tell?

- Our visit to the Louvre
- Our first train ride
- Going snorkeling
- Setting up our camping tent
- Our fancy night out
- Going to a nightclub
- Participating in the circus show
- A cooking class in Provence
- Shopping in a Tokyo department store
- First time in the theme park
- Taking a guided tour of Yosemite Valley
- Learning to waterski
- Fishing in the lake
- Going on a horseback ride
- Playing a board game in a public square in Rome
- The monuments we saw today

You get the idea. Think about your destination or the activities you'll be involved in, and look for what's unique about it, or what people would want to see more of.

245. SILLY PICTURES. Do you know those cheesy pictures where Italian tourists pretend to hold up the Tower of Pisa? If you're in a destination where that's possible — *sorry, I have to say it* — do that. Point to the top of the Eiffel Tower. Pretend to be terrorized by the stuffed grizzly bear in the Anchorage airport. If you're traveling with a group or family, have everyone take that same picture. Trust me, as many beautiful pictures as you'll have, the silly ones will be just as memorable to you as the serious ones.

246. SILLY PICTURE CONTEST. Have everyone in your group take the silliest, funniest picture they can think of, then have a contest to determine the winner. You might enlist a hotel or hospitality person as the contest judge. If you want multiple winners, pick several categories for the winners. For example, "Most Creative Use of a Local Prop," "Best Scenery," and "Most Comical."

247. YEAR AFTER YEAR. If you return to a location year after year, photograph the changes you notice over time. Have new trees been planted? Has the beach changed? Has a new hotel wing been built? Are the restaurants different? Is there more snow this year than last? If so, capture photos of things that are different. This can be a great way to engage the observational skills of young travelers.

248. COMPARED TO HOME. Take photos of stores, objects, cars, or other things you might have at home. How is McDonald's in Spain different than the one at home? What's unique about a Starbucks in Paris? Aside from stores, also look at cars and trucks. Are they bigger? Smaller? Consider also the size of hotel rooms. You might document in pictures how your hotel room in Amsterdam is slightly smaller than a Hyatt in Houston.

249. FIND A NEW ANGLE. Look for a unique aspect of your photographic subject. Most people tend to take pictures of the London Eye or Parthenon in the same way. And yes, do get the traditional photo. But go beyond that. Find something else interesting to document. What's floating in the Seine River? Where does the base of the Eiffel Tower meet the ground? What does a corner of the Empire State Building look like? What does the sand in Amalfi look like? Finding new angles will greatly enrich your photography.

SOUNDS LIKE VACATION

250. CAPTURE SOUNDS TOO. We typically think of photos as the only way to document our vacation travels. But what if, in addition to your thousands of photos, you also recorded audio that conveys the auditory experience of your trip? What might you record?

- Beach waves rolling onto the shore
- Summer rain falling in an Alaska forest
- The roar of Niagra Falls
- Paris street café ambiance

- The bustle of Times Square
- The rushing ocean from your ship balcony
- Disneyland's 9 p.m. fireworks show

You might think these things could just as easily be captured on video. However, audio is a different experience. When you re-watch a vacation video, you are likely engaged with the visual imagery, not the sound. At the top of the Empire State Building, you are going to take in the stunning vistas, the sites you can see. But will you listen to the sounds? You will if you take a sample recording of the destination.

For example, if you're enjoying a street cafe in Lisbon, pull out your phone and record a minute of the sounds around you. Label this recording. And in the future, if you want to remind yourself of the experience, pull out your phone and play "Lisbon cafe," and find yourself transported back to that experience.

251. SUCCESS SOUNDS LIKE... If you do something meaningful on your trip, record the sounds of your triumph, both the ambiance of the moment and your reaction. Perhaps you climbed to the top of Machu Picchu. Record the moment you reached the summit, as well as your thoughts on this accomplishment. Or maybe you just stood up on a paddleboard for the first time and managed to glide a few yards. Let out a holler of joy and ask someone to use your phone to record the sound of your triumph.

252. YOUR VACATION SONG. What music is popular while you're on vacation? If there's a song that stands out, take note. If your vacation was a James Bond movie, perhaps that song would be in the opening title sequence. Years after your trip, hearing that song can take you back to specific moments of your vacation.

When I was flying through London's Heathrow Airport in 2006, I remember hearing the song "Crazy" from the group Gnarls Barkley. Aside from being a catchy song, it also became a touchstone part of the trip. Now when I hear it, I'm taken back to my 2006 travel memories.

253. YOUR PLAYLIST. You might also curate a playlist of songs you listen to on vacation. Maybe they're popular songs of the time. Or maybe they are associated with the destination you're visiting. Or maybe they just give you a specific feeling.

For example, every time I go skiing, I'll make sure there's at least one ski run where I play the James Bond theme as I'm slushing down the slope. Hearing that music makes me feel like I'm 007 in *The Spy Who Love Me*, outracing the bad guys on the Austrian Alps. (To be clear, the music I hear is not the cheesy disco-Bond theme used in the movie.)

SHOPPING FOR THE RIGHT SOUVENIRS

There's a reason airports are filled with souvenir shops. Many of us leave the souvenir shopping until 15 minutes before our flight departs. (My hand is raised; is yours?)

However, now that you're reading this paragraph, you may want to give more thought to the shopping experience, so you don't end up with a bag full of gifts bearing the phrase "...And All I Got Was This Lousy T-Shirt." This next section will help you decide who to shop for and what to get.

254. THE GIVING SPIRIT. Before you buy a single souvenir, you have to get your head right. Do you know the reason why most all souvenir shops are in the airport? One word: guilt. Yes, we've been trained to feel guilty if we go on vacation and don't bring back trinkets for the people in our life. This creates a "have to" mentality when it comes to gift-giving. As in, "I have to get something for so-and-so."

This makes sense, in a way. We went on this big fancy vacation, taking a week and spending thousands of dollars on ourselves. So the least we could do is buy that $14 purple glass tchotchke in Cancun for Aunt Tiffany. Do you see the problem with that statement? Aunt Tiffany is now a "have to," not a "want to."

So the first step in souvenir giving, as we explore it further, is to start by asking one question of every potential gift, for every person: do I *want* to give this, or do I *have* to give this? If it's the latter, maybe adjust your mindset. As much as possible, limit your souvenir gifts to meaningful choices for people who will genuinely appreciate the thought.

255. START WITH A LIST. The first step is to develop a written list of who you want to buy gifts for. I recommend starting with a list of 3–5 people. And yes, I said written. If you only keep it in your head, you're less likely to stick to the plan. Next, consider what those people might like. If you know they have a particular interest or hobby, write that

down. Ideally, you do this step at the beginning of your trip, so you can be open to finding items along the way.

For example, maybe you know Aunt Jane collects plates. Or your friend Mark likes hot sauce. Or your father has a collection of golf shirts from his travels. Knowing this, you can be on the lookout for just the right gift to bring back. You might see a pretty plate Jane would love. A bottle of pepper-infused olive oil is perfect for Mark. And your dad will treasure a golf shirt from the course near your Maui condo. Be creative. With a little advance thought, and a willingness to keep your eyes open, you'll return with a souvenir more prized than the typical box of airport macadamia nut caramels.

256. LET THE KIDS SHOP TOO. Allow your kids to make their own souvenir buying decisions. Ask them at the start of the trip who's on their list — likely it will be school friends, but you never know. Give them a budget and encourage them to make thoughtful decisions using the money they have.

For example, let's say you give them $20 to spend. During the week, if they see something they want to buy, help them understand the cost of that gift relative to their budget. Instead of telling them what to do, ask them questions that encourage them to be smart with their budget. Throughout your vacation, when you shop for souvenirs, help them find fun, creative gifts within their budget.

257. KIDS SOUVENIRS, PART DEUX. Kids have a big advantage over adults. They can draw or color anything at all, and it instantly becomes a treasured gift for the right recipient, such as a grandparent. This can stretch their souvenir budget. For example, they might incorporate their arts or crafts into the gift. Maybe they buy a postcard, and then make a hand-decorated frame with construction paper. Encourage them to connect to what they appreciate about the gift recipient.

258. DO YOU WANT ME TO GET YOU ANYTHING? If you're reading this before you go, ask your friends if there's anything you can bring back. Maybe you're visiting the Vatican, and you have a girlfriend who collects souvenir dessert plates. Ask if she wants you to pick up one with the Pope's face. I'm assuming they exist.

259. SHOP CREATIVELY. Buy things in unexpected places. We're conditioned to think we have to pick up souvenirs from the same old

tried-and-true places. The hotel gift shop. The stands at the airport. But that doesn't have to be. While those purchases do support the local economy, and that's good, you don't have to buy souvenirs in obvious places. Maybe someone you know would like something not considered a souvenir, which you might find in a regular store.

Here's an example. Instead of buying a shirt at the airport that says, "Los Angeles," why not pick up a shirt from an iconic business in Los Angeles, like Randy's Donuts, The Spot in Hermosa Beach, or In-N-Out Burger. Or if you're in Hawaii, get a hat from Cheeseburger in Paradise, Sam Choy's, or Kauai Coffee Company.

With this approach, you're supporting smaller businesses, as opposed to the giant conglomerates that stock the hotel and airport shops.

260. SHOP AT FARMER'S MARKETS. Many cities and towns have weekly farmer's markets with local vendors. You might find the perfect souvenir at one of these stands. Things like jars of local jams, relishes, or salsas. You might be concerned about the weight or bulk of buying items like this, especially if you have lots of travel left before you return home. In this case, you could find a local UPS or FedEx shop, and send the items to your home.

261. ANTIQUE SHOPPING. If you're in a destination where it's easy to find an antique or curio store, look for souvenirs there. Often for a small amount of money, you can find older items that would be perceived as more valuable to the recipient.

This can be especially fun if you're in a foreign or exotic location and the antique items are not only from a different time but a completely different culture. If it's an item you're not familiar with, learn about its purpose, so you can share that with the recipient.

262. SHOP IN PUBLIC MUSEUMS. Consider buying souvenirs in public museums, especially if your purchase will help support their mission. For example, buying a plush bear in the Smithsonian supports them, buying one in the airport doesn't.

263. FREE IS GOOD. Try to find one souvenir for free. Yes, you can buy things. But you could find things along the way that cost you nothing. Can something free still be perceived as valuable? Absolutely! It might take some creativity, but it can be done.

You could easily give items like restaurant recipes, an autograph from a performer, a small scoop of the local sand, a casino chip (small denomination), a local coin or small bill, a drink recipe from your favorite bar, the free museum guide, a guitar pick from the local band you saw, cafe menus or drink glasses. You get the idea. And by the way, nobody must know it was free.

Quick note. Before taking something, ask permission. If the thing you want isn't available, ask if there's something else they might be willing to give you. Also, some destinations like Hawaii have restrictions on removing flora and fauna, so be sure to follow those. Otherwise, you may end up the victims of an ancient Hawaiian curse like Peter and Bobby Brady in the 1970s show, *The Brady Bunch*.

264. "YOU ACTUALLY MADE THIS?" If you have even a small amount of artistic talent, create a piece of art and bring that home as a souvenir. Most of us may think we couldn't do something like this. I'll be the first to say I'm not artistic. But if you gave me some art paper and a watercolor paint set, I could create a passable "painting" of the sunset, a view of the ocean, or the skyline of San Francisco. Even if it's not Picasso-like, the person I give it to knows I gave more thought to this gift than something I picked up at the airport.

265. GIVE THE GIFT OF YOU. Instead of a product, give an experience as a souvenir. For the people in your life you socialize with, consider gifting them experiences inspired by your travels.

You could cook something that brings home a "taste" of your vacation. For example, if I went to Jamaica, I could buy a package of the jerk spice mix. Bringing that home, I would prepare jerk chicken that I serve my guests. The physical item you give as a souvenir would be the wrapped box of spice, with a notecard attached that says, "Good for an evening of Jamaican cuisine."

Another example would be to host a cocktail party with drinks inspired by your vacation destination. The physical "gift" you give people could be a nicely printed card with the drink recipe.

266. WHAT DO YOU WANT? Yes, I'm talking to you now. Collect souvenirs for yourself. We often think of others when we buy souvenirs, but what about us? Do you collect things that are meaningful to you? If not, maybe this is the vacation to start that

practice. If you were going to start a collection, what would it be? See if there's anything on this trip that inspires you to start your collection. Maybe it's the little models of cruise ships. Key chains. Ceramic animals. Glass plates. Baseball caps. Towels. Scarves.

267. ANYTHING CAN BE A SOUVENIR. Collect things we wouldn't normally think of as souvenirs. Things like café napkins, tour maps, beverage cans, and ticket stubs can be fun items to bring home. If you are a scrapbooking person this could be easy for you.

268. FRAME YOUR COLLECTIBLES. If you collect similar objects from your travels, creatively organize them. For instance, if you collect a small amount of beach sand or ground soil from each place you visit, you could place them in a frame, jar, vial, or Christmas ornament. Label each sample with the date and location of your visit. As advised above, only take something from your location if it's permissible.

269. POSTCARDS FROM PARADISE. With the advent of social media, people mail fewer postcards when they travel. But with personal letters becoming more of a rarity, sending postcards to friends and family can be an even more thoughtful and appreciated gesture. But if you're like me, the process of writing cards, however well-intentioned, can seem like a hassle. Make it easier by deciding in advance who's on your list. Then print their address labels on stickers before you go. This way, you just place the sticker on the postcard along with a stamp.

270. MAIL YOURSELF A CARD. You might also consider sending postcards to yourself or your family. If you're touring in a location that has something memorable, get a postcard from that place and send it to yourself. Maybe in the notes section, write your thoughts about what you are seeing. Remind your "home" self how much you enjoyed the trip. Believe me, they'll appreciate it.

GET CREATIVE

271. START A VACATION JOURNAL. Do you keep a journal at home? If so, you might consider keeping a separate vacation journal. This might be a different book you purchase just for the trip, to document the things you see, do, and experience. You don't even have to buy a journal. You could print blank vacation journal pages at home. Bring the pages with you and fill them out.

When you return home, place the pages in a notebook or keepsake box. If you have kids, the upside to this method is that loose pages will be easier to copy or scan and give to them when they're adults. If you're reading this before you go, download my free PDF journal page at www.bestvacationeverbook.com.

272. THERE'S AN APP FOR THAT. If you're more of a digital person, you might instead use an app like Day One or Evernote to record your trip memories. The upside of this approach is you can easily add pictures, timestamps, and voice recordings to your journal entries.

273. WHAT WILL I WRITE ABOUT? What kinds of things can you document in your journal? Consider these prompts:

- Statistics like the weather, sunrise, sunset, etc.
- How much you slept
- What you did today
- Where you ate; what you had to drink
- Things you saw and your impressions
- Things you bought
- What you did the most
- First-time experiences
- Favorite experiences
- Interesting people you met or spoke to
- Inspired thoughts or ideas you had
- Things you didn't have time to see or want to revisit
- Drawings or doodles
- Your favorite drink or meal of the day
- Something that scared you
- Something that surprised you

If you keep a page to summarize your trip, note these topics:

- Favorite aspects of the trip, such as food, museums, people
- The most interesting person you met or conversations you had
- One highlight or memory from each person you traveled with
- The most expensive thing you bought
- The least costly thing that still gave you pleasure
- The biggest challenge you faced
- The biggest surprise you experienced
- Next time you're here you will...

When you get home, print out your favorite 10–20 pictures and put them in this notebook. If you have a binder dedicated just to this trip, decorate the spine and put it on your bookshelf.

274. KIDS JOURNAL. In addition to the journal you create, give your kids a page for their impressions of the trip. Depending on their age, you can offer to help. Keep the questions simple. Ask them what they loved about the day. What was their favorite thing? What activities did they like the most? What was their favorite meal?

275. BECOME A TRAVEL BOOK AUTHOR. Pretend you're a travel journalist like Rick Steves, Pauline Frommer, Angel Castellanos, or Samantha Brown. You want to convince people why they should visit this destination. You've been here for a week. You've seen and done things. So take the essence of your experience and your unique point of view, and share it with the world.

Where do you start? Write a post on social media or record a video. If audio is your thing, create a recording on your smartphone. None of this has to be perfect. Just capture the essence of your experience. You don't even have to share it. Just keep it for yourself.

276. HIT THE "RECORD" BUTTON. Create a recording on your smartphone in which you share your experiences, insights, and what moved you about this trip. Imagine having the opportunity to "playback" the impressions of your travels over the years. This can be especially meaningful if you return to this destination in the future. For example, if you go to the same time-share each year, that aspect won't change. But your perspectives each year can be different. It's worth documenting how you change over time.

277. GET A KID'S POINT OF VIEW. Interview your kids about the trip by using your smartphone to record their thoughts. You could do this on video, though older kids may be self-conscious, and only want audio. Not to worry. If you want to share this with them, you can still make a movie compilation with their voiceover, accompanied by pictures you take.

Ideally, ask them the same questions each time you travel. The value of this is that, over time, you'll hear their views evolve on this subject. Ask questions like, "What's your favorite part of the trip?" and "What did you love seeing?"

278. DO AN A.M.A. If you're engaged in social media like Facebook or Instagram, conduct an A.M.A, or Ask Me Anything. Find out what your friends want to know about your destination. Maybe it's the cost of admission for the Space Needle, the water temperature in Maine, when the set sets in Juneau in June, or the cost of a local babysitter. The process of researching these questions can be a fun way to learn more about your destination, and help you engage with people you meet along the way. Of course, you may not be able to answer every question. In cases where you're stumped, you can reply to the question with a selfie of you shrugging!

279. CREATE ART. In addition to journaling or documenting your thoughts on audio, you can create art. Now you might argue you're not an artist. Who cares! Do kids in grade school ever say they aren't artists? Of course not! They create art with whatever they have.

Bring a sketch book or art journal, and colored pencils, and create simple pieces of art while you are traveling. If you have a tablet with an art program, use that. Some programs even allow you to start with a picture you've taken and draw over it.

What will you draw or sketch? Anything! Draw a picture of the view from your room or the view from a park. Make visual maps of the places you see. Draw a picture of yourself in the location.

It doesn't matter what these drawings or pieces of art look like. It's more important that you are finding creative ways to express yourself. Who knows, you might find you like art!

280. TEAM UP FOR ART. Kids don't need encouragement to create art, so they may be ahead of you on this. Consider doing a piece of art together with them. You do some, and they do some.

Depending on their age, encourage them to "direct" your involvement. Ask them to tell you what to do. They'll love that. A piece of art you create together can be a vacation treasure you'll always remember.

TAKE MEMORIES, LEAVE NOTHING ELSE

281. NO GRAFFITI PLEASE. Sadly, there are few places in the world you can travel where you don't see instances of people having graffitied their initials into a setting. Sigh... Please don't be the person

who does this. Instead, think about non-permanent ways to leave your imprint, after which you snap a photo for posterity:

- If you're at the beach, write your initials and the year in the sand
- If you're in the snow, build a snowman and let "him" hold a sign
- Use elements from nature like flower petals to write your initial.

282. "X" MARKS YOUR SPOT, WHERE "X" IS TEMPORARY. Create a "faux" set of initials. If you're in an urban setting, use construction paper to make a "marker" with your initials. Wherever you go, place this marker on a tree with tape, with your destination in the background. Snap a photo, take down your marker, and move on.

283. "WE WERE HERE." Make a vacation plaque. Create a printed page (at home) with the dates and location of your trip. At each significant location, take a picture of yourself with your marker.

284. DORA THE EXPLORER. If your child has a favorite stuffed animal or action figure, take pictures of this toy "visiting" each location. Depending on the age of your child, this toy may not be in favor (or even survive) for more than a year or two. If that's the case, be happy your child will at least have those memories. You might persuade older kids to carry on the tradition of bringing that toy on vacation. Yes, I realize a 14-year-old might not want to travel with the Dora the Explorer doll they loved at age 6. But it's worth asking.

285. MEET OUR MASCOT. Along the lines of kids with stuffed animals or toys, consider "adopting" a family mascot or good luck charm that travels with you on vacation. Maybe this mascot is related to your family name or heritage. For example, as someone named Thor, I might carry a Thor action figure who could travel the world with me and pose for pictures in various locations.

286. IMPROVE THE WORLD. Leave things better than you found them. If the opportunity exists, contribute to the improvement of your destination. There are several ways to do this. You might look for an opportunity to volunteer for a charity or non-profit. Perhaps there's a local shelter you could assist for an hour. You might also look for an environmental group that does a beach or park cleanup.

287. PAY IT FORWARD. If you know this destination well, either because you've been there a while, or because it's an old favorite,

offer your expertise to someone who's just arriving, or has never been there before. This can be especially helpful if you've got tips, tricks, or first-hand knowledge that would benefit someone else.

288. DONATE TO OTHERS. If you've acquired things like pool rafts, floaties, or other items you won't use at home, or don't want to take with you, give them to someone else. On our visits to Hawaii, this has become a custom of our final day at the beach. That $2.99 inflatable raft that's wet and sandy? We find someone who looks like they'd appreciate it and offer it to them. They love it and we feel great.

THINK EXPERIENCE FIRST

289. DO SOMETHING WORTH REMEMBERING. This might seem self-evident. You're on vacation, of course, that's worth remembering. But think back to all the trips you've even been on. Do they all blend in? What moments separate them from one another?

Sometimes these moments will happen spontaneously. You might attend a show that involves audience participation, and you get called up on stage to be part of the act. Of course, you'll remember this experience. You couldn't have anticipated it, but it will be part of your treasured vacation memories.

If you haven't yet experienced a moment like this, consider making one. Maybe it's doing something that takes you out of your comfort zone, like jumping off a bluff into the ocean. Or perhaps it's having dinner on the beach at sunset. Or it might be going to a school, bringing a backpack filled with supplies, and reading to the kids.

Whatever you choose, ask yourself, will this experience stand the test of time, and become a memory I love sharing with others? If so, make that memory.

6

WHAT IF…

27 Ways to Go from Dream Trip to Dream Life

As you read this, you may be nearing the end of your vacation. The end. Of your vacation. My apologies for typing that.

Here you are, feeling all connected and recharged. And then Thor has to point out vacations don't go on forever. It would be great if they did, wouldn't it? But the sad truth is, most of us don't have $7.5 million in savings, so "forever vacations" aren't an option. Though I am working on the millions part.

So yes, nobody likes to see their vacation end. Why is that? Hopefully, it's because you're having an amazing time and you love being in this place with your traveling companions, or the friends you met along the way.

With your vacation time ending, you'll soon return to "normal life," however you define that. Now if you're like most people, you may not be fully in love with that normal life. If so, relax, this is the right chapter for you.

You may have heard the phrase "dream vacation." Most of us would define a "dream vacation" as a vacation one could only dream about but rarely got the chance to experience. Was this a dream vacation for you? I hope it was.

If you picked some of the exercises to do each day, hopefully it has opened your eyes to a different way of living your life, at least when you are on vacation. You could, if you choose, apply that same thinking when you return home.

You probably have also heard the phrase "dream life." Most of us would define a "dream life" as a life in which everything went amazingly well. We got to experience the best of everything, and never had any challenges or problems. That's not reality. But what if it was?

What if you woke up every day and said, "I love my life!" You love the experience of being you, the opportunities you have, the relationships that you enjoy, and the difference you get to make in the world.

Does this sound impossible? Maybe the "you" before vacation might have answered yes. But what about the "you" that's now on vacation? Do you feel different? Perhaps more relaxed, happier, more optimistic, more rested? If so, good!

That is a great place from which to look at who you are and decide if there are things you can do to make the rest of your life more like a vacation. Let's jump into today's A.O.'s...

GO ON VACATION AGAIN

290. WHAT DID I LOVE? In a moment, I will encourage you to think about your next vacation or travel experience. But before we do that, let's celebrate this trip. Let's document what's been truly great. Don't just think about it casually for half a second, like, "Oh yeah, I liked that thing. That other thing was fun too. Okay, I'm done, moving on." NO! Take the time to write down the moments you loved about this vacation. Why do we do this?

For one thing, years from now you might not remember all these specific moments. Believe me, you'll appreciate having taken the time to record them while they are still fresh in your memory.

Also, writing down what you loved will help you choose what you want to do in the future. Maybe you write down that you loved sitting by the pool reading an inspiring book. That was my experience years ago. Knowing that I can curate future travel opportunities with more of these kinds of experiences.

So take out your vacation journal (or whatever you use) and write down at least TEN things you loved about this trip. They could be experiences, moments, people you met, meals you enjoyed, fun things you did, a particular sunset, a great insight you had, a new thing you tried, a bond you strengthened, whatever. Write it down. If you come up with more than ten, great!

291. WHAT DIDN'T I LOVE? Okay, let me be super clear here. I'm not asking you to write down what you didn't love, despite the heading. Not at all. I do not want you to focus on what you didn't like. I do not want you to focus on the bad experiences or things that didn't go well.

Instead, I want you to focus on what you learned, or what you could do differently next time. In other words, don't list the things you didn't like. Take responsibility for those situations and decide you will use them to have a better experience next time. It's a subtle distinction. But when we list things we didn't like, we may be in blame mode. Like, "It's the hotel's fault my room wasn't ready... It's the restaurant's fault the service was slow.... It's the ship's fault for not having any spa appointments."

But you know what? We were the common denominator in all those situations. You and I. So WE could've done something differently. We could've done more research. We could've chosen a different time to eat. We could've booked our appointment sooner. Instead of saying what you didn't love, write down what you learned or what you would do differently next time.

292. WHERE TO NEXT? Before you leave, let's start thinking about your next vacation. Yes, I said *next* vacation. The first question to ask is, would you come back here in a year? (If you've visited several places on this trip, think about the one that stood out most.) If you wouldn't return to this exact place, what would you do differently? Would you visit a new location? Would you stay in different accommodations? Write in your vacation journal what you would do differently. Feeling inspired, perhaps write, "A year from now, I will .... "

293. BE YOUR TRAVEL AGENT. If you could see returning to this destination, but maybe in a new way, take a sneak peek of the other options. Experience what it feels like to be in that setting. Immerse yourself. Listen to the sounds, and take in the visuals.

For example, let's say I'm winding down a trip to Vienna. Maybe I stayed in an American-style hotel on this trip, but I'm open to trying something different.

Perhaps a boutique-style property in a different district. If so, I could go there now and explore, to see if it's a place I would even like. I might take pictures of myself at the hotel. I'll make notes about what I love. I could check out the surrounding area, to see if it's a place I'd want to spend more time. I'd talk to the locals, to get a feel for the area. I'd ask their opinion of the best places to stay, or the restaurants I should try. By doing all of this, I'll have a better sense of the area.

294. PUTTIN' ON THE RITZ. Since this is all just for fun, why not imagine your next trip as something bigger or nicer? We're just dreaming here, right? Nothing is set in stone. We're just thinking about where we *might* go next time. Why not up-level your imagination?

For example, if I'm on vacation in Miami, and I'm staying in a downtown hotel because that fits my budget, I could explore what it would be like to stay in Miami Beach next time. I know this might *currently* be outside my budget range. But that's okay. This imaginary trip is a year (or more) away, and I'm just dreaming now.

An afternoon spent there — exploring hotels, restaurants, the street life — could be time well spent. Take pictures of yourself there. Stop by restaurants and check out the menus. Imagine what you'd order for dinner. Sit by the pool at the hotel, walk to the beach, and enjoy a drink at sunset. Soak in the feeling of actually staying here. You never know what the future holds!

COULD YOU IMAGINE LIVING HERE?

295. ADDRESS FORWARDING. It's a vacation cliché that when you're having an amazing time on vacation, people often imagine themselves moving to this destination permanently. I can't tell you how many times in my twenties I imagined selling everything and becoming a G.O. (staff person) at Club Med. I never did this, but the romance of the idea always excited me.

Ask yourself with this particular trip, would you move here if you could? Dig further into this idea. Ask what is it about this place that intrigues you. Many of us might answer, "I like the idea of drinking piña coladas at the pool all day long." (I'm sad to say, that is now the last piña colada reference in the book.)

Obviously you couldn't live this lifestyle if you worked there. But you might find there's something else about this place that appeals to you. If so, write it down. In your vacation journal, you might write, "If I lived here, I would .... "

296. SERIOUSLY, THOUGH... Okay, if you really could see yourself living here, and the prospect feels slightly realistic, learn what it's like to live here. If you haven't met anybody during your stay that works at this location, find someone to interview. Tell them you want the pros and cons. Here are some questions you might ask:

- Is it easy to get a job here?
- Where do people live?
- How far away from work do they live?
- What's an average workweek like?
- What does it cost to live here?

You may not find people willing to share specifics on all these questions. But you can gather bits and pieces, here and there, to give you a better perspective on living like a local.

If you don't have enough time to follow through on this (after all, you might not be reading this until Day 6 or 7), exchange contact info with someone you meet on vacation. Or ask for their social media handle. You could follow someone on Instagram or Twitter, and then private message them later as questions occur to you.

297. THE KIDS ARE MOVING HERE! Ask your kids to describe what they imagine life would be like if they lived here. This isn't likely to be realistic, especially if your children are super young. Their conception of living here could be "working" by the pool all the time and having fun. That's okay. Explore the possibility without judgment.

Ask what kind of job they might have if they lived here. What would they love to do? Who would they be friends with? Write down their answers in your vacation journal.

If they're willing, record the conversation on video. If done throughout their childhood and edited together, they could watch this one day and see how their "dream life" evolved.

298. GET A CARD. If you're even halfway serious about the possibility of living here, get a business card from a location specialist or realtor. We've probably all traveled to locations and seen real estate offices for that destination. If you're passing by one, grab a card or snap a photo of their contact info.

Once you get home, check them out online. Decide to periodically contact them to learn more about the destination. If your interest develops into a serious pursuit, let them know. Tell them your dream property and ask them to alert you when they find it.

LIVE BY DESIGN

299. FINISH STRONG. Was there something you started on vacation you haven't finished? Did you have an intention you haven't followed through on? If so, decide that before you go home, you'll finish and follow through to the extent that's possible. Maybe you started a book on the trip. Finish it before you go home, assuming that's practical, and assuming you still like it. Here are some other possible things you may have considered over the last week, but put off:

- Do that run-on-the-beach, stand-up paddleboard, or whatever activity that captivates you
- Create a smartphone photo album for your vacation pictures (see #228–233)
- Journal about your experiences
- Find someone who made your vacation better and thank them
- Take some alone time to enjoy your environment
- Pick up that last-minute souvenir
- Go dancing with your spouse

Bottom line: was there something you considered doing, but didn't because you were afraid? Do it now! Finish strong!

300. KEEP IT GOING. Imagine for a moment it's the first few days back from vacation. You've done your laundry, sorted the mail, and filled up the fridge. Things are back to normal.

But your definition of normal doesn't have to mean the same thing as it did before vacation. Your life could be different. If things were going well on vacation, keep that good feeling going.

Resolve that before you return home, you'll carry over one thing you did on vacation, and do it for an entire week. *Yes, you might form a new habit.* Let's say there's an activity you've enjoyed on vacation. If it's something you can continue at home, decide you'll continue when you get home.

Right now, at this moment, you could set a goal to change one habit before returning home, to continue for one week. Make it something you can do both on vacation and at home. If you're reading this on the way home, or at home, you can just as easily start your seven-day clock now. Start today!

For example, if you walked every day on vacation, decide you will walk for one week — seven days — when you get home. Make it easy. If you walked for an hour every day on vacation, then yes, continue that habit. But make the goal easier. Can you walk for 10–15 minutes at home? If so, make that your "keep it going" goal.

301. MAKE IT RIDICULOUS. If you skipped past the exercise above, even though part of you thought it sounded worthwhile, STOP! Ask yourself: did you avoid deciding because there was something about the goal that seemed too difficult? If so, make it smaller and easier. In short, make it ridiculous. What do I mean by this? Make it something so ridiculously easy to do you couldn't possibly NOT do it.

Look, I get we all want to do big, meaningful things in life. We've been conditioned to think massive goals are the way to go. There's value in this, but not if that goal becomes the reason you don't take action.

Let's say I decide I'm going to return home and swim every day for a week. Maybe I swam in the ocean every day on vacation, and it seems like a worthwhile goal to continue. But unless I have an ocean in my backyard, this goal might not be practical.

In my case, I could make it easier and say, I'll go swim in the pool at the gym for seven days. But even that goal may encounter resistance. It's too easy to come up with excuses. *The gym is too far. I'll have to change and shower afterward. What if the lanes are crowded?*

The solution, at least for these seven days, is to make your goal ridiculously simple to achieve. Make it easy on yourself. If walking 10 minutes every day is your goal, then make that simpler. Decide you'll only have to walk 5 minutes every day.

Bottom line: don't give yourself any excuses to not continue what you started on vacation. Here are some other examples:

If you did yoga every day on vacation, a ridiculously easy way to keep it going is to do one pose per day for 7 days. Do triangle. Do mountain. Do downward dog. Just one.

If you meditated for 20 minutes, a ridiculously easy way to keep it going is to sit down for 2 minutes, every day, and focus on your breath. *Are you kidding? I can do that.*

If you did 10 pushups and 10 sit-ups every day on vacation, a ridiculously easy way to keep it going is to...do 10 pushups and 10 sit-ups. I mean, seriously, 10 and 10 isn't that hard to keep going, is it? So do that! Or if you must, do 9 and 9.

The easier the goal, the more likely you'll do it. And if you do it consistently, you might find you like it, and it might become, dare I say, a habit you enjoy.

By the way, I just have to say, I was so excited when I wrote #300. We made it through 300 travel tips and suggestions. Way to go, us! And now, to paraphrase the late Casey Kasem, back to the countdown....

302. KID HABITS. Ask your kids if there's one new thing they might be willing to do when they get home. What's a new habit they might adopt? Avoid telling them what you think they should do. You've probably got a long list of those, right? Brush your teeth, wash your face, wear your retainer, make your bed, clean up your room, get off the XBOX — ohmygod, I sound like a parent!

The point is, ask them what they think. This will give you insights as to what they consider important. Whatever they decide, support them. They might not choose what you want. But they're more likely to follow through if it matters to them. And the real benefit is they'll develop confidence in their own ability to take action.

303. ONE MORE THING. Aside from adopting a new habit that you (or your kids) have decided to continue for seven days, is there anything else you enjoyed doing this week, that you might like to try

again at home? Was there one tip, game, or strategy you had fun with, or that enthralled you? If so, consider doing it at home.

Maybe your family really enjoyed having dinner together and talking about your day. Now, this might not be something you will do for seven days in a row. That might not be practical. But you could do it once a week. Try it out and see.

304. DO MORE BEFORE 9 A.M. The US Army ran a TV commercial in the 1980s that promised you could "be all that you can be" if you joined the Army. "We do more before 9 a.m. than most people do all day." Starting your day with significant accomplishments does have a certain appeal.

If you still haven't figured out an activity you want to continue, or even if you have, consider designing an ideal morning routine. A set of activities you do every morning, no matter what. Think of it as a way to start your day on your terms, doing things that set you up to win. Pick 2–3 activities meaningful to you, then decide to do them every day for the next week.

What might you choose? Perhaps meditation, prayer, journaling, expressing gratitude, light stretching, or reading. Keep it simple and easy to accomplish. Don't go overboard and overcommit.

Think about your typical morning. However much time you can consistently commit, do that. If it's fifteen minutes, then use that time for your three activities, five minutes each.

For example, do five minutes of meditation or prayer, followed by five minutes of listing all the things you're grateful for, then five minutes of reading an inspiring book. Do this, and you'll be more likely to go through your day feeling like it's a vacation.

305. SEVEN DAYS FROM NOW. You've now decided what you'll do when you return home. Let's make sure you follow through.

Set an appointment with yourself for Seven Days From Now. (Yes, I meant to capitalize those words, thereby making them a Proper Noun. You see, people take Proper Nouns much more seriously. Also when things are capitalized, it means they are important.)

So you'll make an appointment for Seven Days From Now, or whatever date will be seven days after you've been home. Go ahead and take out your phone... *I'll wait...* *Okay good.*

Make a ten-minute appointment called, "Follow Up." During this appointment, you'll answer for yourself three questions:

1) What one thing did I decide to do every day when I got home?

2) Did I do it?

3) If not, why?

Okay, forget question number three. The answer to question #2 must be "yes." Therefore, there isn't an "If not, why?" option. *You will do it, right?* Good. If you move beyond this sentence without making the appointment, hmm, what can I say besides, I STRONGLY recommend you not give yourself the excuse. Make the appointment. Do the thing.

306. YOUR VACATION ANNIVERSARY. Before going home, set a date for a Vacation Anniversary celebration. *What? You've never heard of a Vacation Anniversary?* It's totally a thing, I promise.

It's where you set a date for 2–3 weeks after your vacation ends, and you plan fun games and activities to celebrate your vacation and the amazing experience you had. "Oh yes, now I know what you're talking about," you say. "I've totally heard of that... No, actually I haven't. But I am interested." Great!

So what can you do on a Vacation Anniversary? (Note I did the All Caps thing again. That's how you know it's real.) Here's a few ideas:

- If you created a vacation playlist, tell Alexa to crank up the tunes. (See #253)
- If you have a favorite set of vacation pics on your phone, scroll through them
- If you recorded sounds of your vacation, like the sound of waves, listen to the clips.
- Did you have a favorite drink while on vacation? "Toast" your trip by recreating it.
- Was there a vacation meal that stood out? If so, recreate that culinary experience.

- Was there an activity you enjoyed, such as a board game? If so, play that.
- If you made any new friends on vacation and exchanged addresses, consider writing them a "Thinking of You" postcard to see how they're doing. If you only have their social media handle, send them a direct message.
- If you kept a journal, review your entries. If doing this as a family, share your favorite memories. Has anything changed since the trip? Were your favorites then still your favorites now?

If this sounds fun, pick a day 2–3 weeks after your vacation ends, and make it your Vacation Anniversary celebration. Calendar it now!

307. BE MORE SOCIAL. I probably don't have to suggest that you post vacation photos on social media. Everyone does that. Go deeper. Update your profile on your preferred social platform. Add an insight or two that you learned on this trip. Again, I'm not saying post your drink or sunset pictures. Rather, post your thoughts on what you learned while on this trip. What surprised you? Who were you delighted to meet? What was your favorite experience?

Now go to your profile page. Under "About," consider if you might amend who you are. Yes, you might return home and still be an "IT Engineer," "Homemaker," "Sales VP" or whatever it is you do during the day. But is there a more playful way to describe that? Is there a more expansive definition for what it is you do? If so, consider changing what you call yourself. It's just a simple social media account. One change made there doesn't hurt, right?

IMAGINE A DIFFERENT YOU

308. ONE QUALITY TO IMPROVE. When you think about your many qualities — both great and not-so-great — is there one aspect you'd like to change? Maybe there's one quality you want to increase. Or maybe a behavior you'd like to decrease.

Let's say you think of yourself as a generally patient person, but you want to display more patience. Decide to emphasize that quality in your life. Remind yourself of this each day with an affirmation like, "I bring more patience to each moment of my day." Or if you want to decrease a current behavior, you can do this same thing, just state the reverse of it.

For example, if I tend to get easily distracted during my day, I will decide to strive for the opposite of distraction. I could say "I bring focus and clarity to each moment of my day." Pick one quality to focus on the first week you're back. If you try to do too much, you may burn out and give up.

Be easy on yourself. You may not be perfect, but if you set an intention to focus each day on this one quality, you're more likely to anchor that into your default personality.

309. DOUBLE DOWN ON GREATNESS. Another way to look at self-improvement is to think about something you're already good at doing, then do more of it. Take your best quality and double down on it. This might be a personal quality to focus on, or a skill to highlight.

For example, maybe I consider myself to be a decent speaker. I enjoy talking to people, I feel comfortable speaking. It's one of my assets. So why not take that strength and emphasize it more? I could look to improve even more, read a book on speaking, take a course, or join Toastmasters. I'm starting with something I'm naturally good at, and I'm applying deliberate effort to make myself even better.

Another way to think of this is to pick a skill or hobby you have, something you love doing, and ask if it can become a more prominent part of your life. A skill could become a hobby; a hobby could become a passion; a passion could become a side business, or a side business could become a full-time job.

For example, you might love crafts projects like woodworking or pottery making. Perhaps if you spent more time on that, you might see ways to turn this into a bigger hobby that might eventually become a business or even a career. Start by asking yourself, what do I love? What am I already good at? What do people praise me for? Next ask, what *more* could I do with that? Have fun exploring the answers that come to you.

310. LEVEL UP A WEAKNESS. An alternative to doubling down on strength is to find an area of your life that's not currently your forte and decide to improve there. This might be something you know you should do. You've been thinking about it for a while. Maybe it's exercise. Or meditation. Or gaining more clients for your business. Increasing your income. Paying off debts.

Maybe it's something simple, like making your bed or flossing once a day. Whatever it is, you believe that doing it will improve your life. If you know there's a weakness you have in a certain area, decide to address it before going home. Make one decision on what you can do. Then do it.

311. BE IN THE MOMENT. It's one thing to want to improve. But our lives are lived in dozens of moments every single day. You move from one activity to another. You make decisions about what to do, what to eat, what to say, and what to focus on. But here's my question. Are you being intentional with those decisions? For most of us, the answer is "not enough." So what if you decided to be more intentional, to bring more focus to your individual moments each day?

Author and coach Brendon Burchard offers a two-step process to improve our mindfulness as we move from one activity to another. In *High Performance Habits*, he suggests we first take a minute or two to release our focus on whatever activity has just ended. Literally say the word "release" as you let go of any tension in your mind and body. When you feel the tension subsiding, you next set the intention of what you want to achieve or experience in the next moment of your life. You might ask, "What do I want to bring into this next activity?" or "How can I enjoy the situation more?"

This simple process allows you to change the way you show up in each moment of your life. You bring intention and focus to what you do and who you are.

312. HELLO, I AM... Speaking of who you are, have you ever thought of becoming someone else? If so, you might come up with a temporary way to introduce yourself. Imagine you are meeting someone new. They ask what you do. Instead of giving your standard response, you say...*something made up or something fun.* You might resist this. After all, you'd be telling a lie. But think of it as taking a moment to explore creative license.

What would this look like? Well, I could say I'm about to go on a tour with a rock band as their new guitarist. The key is to notice how it feels when you say it. Are you excited, nervous, or intrigued? Does part of you believe it's possible? If so, write down what the moment feels like.

It's possible you feel uneasy because you're lying to a stranger, or you think, what if they ask for the name of my rock band, or if I know Mick or Bruce or Jon? That would be so embarrassing, you might think. If you're concerned, fine, tell the truth. Then blame me. Share that you were playing a game to expand your consciousness.

What if they respond, "Yeah, you had me going. I thought I saw you on the Grammys"? If you hear that, explore this idea further. Maybe some aspect of that identity is in your future, *hmm?*

313. A TWO-MONTH PURPOSE. If pretending to be in a rock band feels uncomfortable, it's probably because that identity is too much of a stretch for you to believe. What if we could make it easier? What if we made it so your mind had no choice but to say, "Yeah, I buy that"? Okay, we're going to trick your mind now, so SHUSHH, don't tell it. *Whispering now...*

When you get home, pick something you can do for TWO MONTHS. There are only three rules. One, it has to be something with a finite completion or event. Two, it has to be fun. And three, it has to be something that can produce a new identity for you.

Some examples: train for a 5K, then run a race. Boom, now you're a runner. Or maybe take singing lessons, then schedule an evening where you belt out one song at a karaoke bar. Now you're a singer. Or learn to sculpt, create a piece of art, and now you're a sculptor. You get the idea.

This example is personal to me. Finishing and publishing this book makes me an author. The editing process took me about — you guessed it — two months. I specifically chose this two-month purpose for myself, so that I could create a new, empowering identify.

So take two months, and create a fun way of seeing yourself.

314. TELL IT TO A STRANGER. Is there some part of your life you want to change? If so, resolve to make that change in the next year. But while you're still on vacation, tell a total stranger. What kind of change am I talking about? It could be anything. Something big, like looking for a new job, or something small, like drinking more water.

You probably have a sense of what you might change. If not, reflect on the thoughts that continually occur to you. If you think about something every day, it means you probably ought to go beyond just thinking about it. You might want to consider action.

How would this work? First, think of an aspect of your life that's up for consideration. Next, find a stranger and tell them your decision.

For example, if you're in a place where they speak a foreign language, and you intend to return here in the future, find someone you think will be here in a year and make a pact with them: the next time you see them, you'll have a conversation in their language. Or if you've decided to look for a new job, tell this stranger you have decided to look for new work.

The beauty of talking to a stranger is you are unlikely to see them again, so... who cares what they think of your decision? Also, you probably don't have to worry about seeing them in the future. So if you didn't end up making that change, they won't be there to judge you. That's kind of liberating, isn't it?

Whatever happens with this decision, there won't be anyone there to judge you, good or bad. So have fun telling a total stranger where you're going in life!

315. A CALL FROM PARADISE. Send yourself a voicemail with a message of encouragement. How will you do this? Borrow somebody's phone, perhaps your spouse or friend's (or maybe even a stranger?)

Call your own cell phone and leave a message that you'll listen to when you get home. In this message, you are talking to yourself. Think of this as "vacation you" supporting or coaching "home you."

It might go something like this:

> "Hey, Thor (your name, obviously, unless you're calling me to encourage me.) I wanted you to know I had an amazing time on this trip. First, I want to thank you for taking me, for all the planning you did, and for the hard work you put in. I had a fantastic time. Thank you so much. Also, I want to tell you how AWESOME you are. You are so smart, fun, and capable. And I know you can do anything you set your mind to. And that idea you had

to — [INSERT IDEA HERE] — that idea is genius. I know you can do that. You will be fantastic. I believe in you. I support you. And I love you. You can do this!"

Yes, something like that. Leave yourself that message. Short and sweet. When you get home, listen to it.

Any time you need a reminder of who you can be, listen to the message. If you need encouragement, listen. If you want a laugh, listen. If you want to remember how happy you were when you are living your best life, listen.

316. CREATE A SYMBOL. If you've decided to take action when you get home, great! Well done you! With that commitment to doing things differently, why not create something as a symbol of that commitment, to carry with you every day for the next week. What might this be? Perhaps a keychain, a piece of jewelry, a stone, or a seashell. It doesn't have to be elaborate or expensive. Just make sure it's something you can wear or carry in your pocket.

Once you have the object that will be your symbol, imbue it with the positive energy of this trip. Find an activity you've enjoyed doing, something that creates warm feelings of love and appreciation. Maybe it's being in nature, on the beach, watching the sunset or the ocean. Wherever you feel awesome, that's the place!

Now take out your symbol, hold it in your hand, and as you let the good feelings of this moment wash over you, focus your attention on this symbol. You are now anchoring those good feelings with that object. When you return home, simply take out the object, and those feelings will come back to you.

DREAM LIFE

317. One of the best things to do on vacation is to imagine what your dream life could look like. The kind of life that, when you go on vacation, it's a celebration, not an escape. I invite you to spend time today — no more than 20 minutes — and focus on creating a life you would love.

Here's exactly how to do this. Find a place where you won't be disturbed. Ideally, it's your happy place. A spot that makes you feel good, that you love, that brings you life.

In this place, with paper and pen, write down three things you were grateful for on this vacation. It can be anything that makes you feel good. If you had a wonderful hike in a beautiful natural setting, write that down. If you had a great meal with someone, write that down. If you saw an awe-inspiring sight, write that down.

As you write, begin each sentence with "I am so grateful for...," then write what you were grateful for in the present tense.

For example, if you were in Paris, you might write, "I am so grateful to see the beauty of Paris from the Eiffel Tower." Emphasize what it *feels* like to be in this experience. Choose memories for which the feelings are strong, and the memories vivid. Make sense? Write down three things you are grateful for on this trip.

Hopefully, you are now in a good feeling place. What you will do next is to pick one area of your life you want to improve. It might be your health and well-being, your relationships, your career, or work, or how you spend your time.

Pick one area, then write down what your life would look like in three years. Why three years? Because that time frame is far enough out that your egoic mind can suspend belief and just play along.

Allow yourself to dream big. Don't worry about how any of this will happen. You are imagining your life without regard for present circumstances. Just write down what you would love.

If time and money weren't an issue, what would you do? What would you be? What would you have? Spend a few minutes imagining.

Here's an example. A dream I came up with was in the area of health. I decided that three years from now, I would like to learn how to surf. It wasn't necessarily because I had always wanted to surf. But I knew that this goal, which sounded like fun, would require me to have a certain level of health and fitness to do it. I would have to be stronger and more flexible. I would need to stretch or do yoga. All these things would put me in a position to surf.

In the dream, I can see myself on a surfboard in Waikiki. I can imagine the warm water, the smell in the air. I can look to my left and see the sun setting over the mountains in Oahu. I want to truly embody this dream, so I add as many sensory experiences as I can, to make it feel as real as possible.

The next step is to look at your dream, in a good feeling state, and brainstorm five to ten things you could do to make this dream a reality. They could be simple things or big things. Just whatever comes to you in this good feeling state, write it down.

Once you have five to ten things, look at your list. Let yourself feel each one, then circle the first three you identify with most.

Of those three, choose one you'll do first. If it's something you can do now, great. If not, put it on your calendar. Pull out your phone right now and write down when you will do this task. Maybe it's making a phone call. Researching something. Whatever it is, decide right now you are going to do that thing at that time.

Congratulations! While on vacation, you took the first step toward the future version of yourself. Anytime you want to do more of this, just repeat these steps!

This may be the end of your vacation, but we'll continue to spend some time together over the next week. So keep reading!

COME BACK NEW

You're on the plane right now. Or in the car. You are heading home. Many of us feel good about that. There are things we miss about being home. Our bed. Our food. Our routines. Our friends.

There are also things you may not miss. Chief among them, your job, email inbox, school, yardwork, housework, racing at 80 mph to get everything done. Yes, you won't miss that.

But you're not home yet. So technically, you are still on vacation. Let's stay in that mindset a little longer.

Being on vacation is an excellent setting to think bigger, more expensive thoughts about your life. Chances are, you are probably happy now. You were just on vacation after all. You are as relaxed as it gets. You feel good about things.

So why not take a moment to imagine the life you return home to being different. You don't have to do everything all at once. You don't have to plow back into "regular you" mode. Pace yourself. Give yourself a break. You were just on vacation. Let that good feeling last a little while. How do we do that? One day at a time. Literally. Starting with your first day back.

Yes, I know. You probably don't want to think about that. Why? Because you can probably imagine it will be stressful returning to your normal routines and responsibilities. You may have to go back to work or school, you've got a suitcase full of laundry to unpack, mail to sort, food to buy.

But just for a moment, imagine if all that work was easy. "How is that possible?" you may ask. I'll tell you!

You've probably heard that experiences only have the meaning we give them. If we decide something is going to be stressful, guess what? It probably will be. Instead, why not decide, right now, that the first day you return home won't be quite so bad.

In fact, maybe it could be, who knows, *great?*

Right now, I want you to make a decision. I want you to decide to be easy on yourself when you get home. For one day. You can decide what to do after that. But for this one day, why not allow yourself to be in semi-vacation mode.

So tomorrow, when you start the next section, you will be home...

PART 2
BACK HOME

7

FIND GRATITUDE AT HOME

You're home. You made it. Home. All the comforts of your own space. If you missed certain things while on vacation (your bed maybe?) now you have them back. Yay, home!

Being home also means, quite obviously, your vacation is over. Sorry to have to write that sentence. Nobody likes to read that. Probably because for most of us, it means 50 weeks until our next vacation.

Most people will read that and their heart will sink. Fifty weeks of the same-old, same-old. But it doesn't have to be that way. That's why you picked up this book. You are creating a new vision for your life.

Let's start with a new way of looking at things. Yes, your vacation is over. But your life is just beginning. A life that doesn't require you to take a vacation as an escape.

With your new way of looking at life, you'll go on vacation not to escape or forget, but to compliment the already exciting, fulfilling, passionate things you do in your everyday life.

If you're someone who enjoys an occasional drink, the analogy I'll make is that instead of thinking of your vacation as a drunken escapade, and your regular life as sobriety; think of vacation as savoring a fine vintage wine and think of your life as the joy-filled effort that creates that vintage and shares it with the world.

TODAY'S FOCUS

318. SAY THANK YOU. On your first day of vacation (remember that?) you made gratitude your primary focus. We talked about centering our

attention on people or things we were grateful for. Today, we have one focus and it's simple.

Your objective is to say "thank you" to three people. It could be the person that holds the door for you. The person who gives you coffee. The office co-worker who says it's nice to have you back. Just find three people today to thank.

Bonus points if the people don't expect it. Enjoy their surprise when you thank them.

You could probably knock this out by 9 a.m. Maybe you say thanks to the barista who hands you coffee. Or the gas station clerk. Or the train ticket taker.

Now, you could do all this and still not feel anything. You won't get those vacation vibes. Why is this? Are you doing it wrong? Of course not. Most likely, you've just settled back into your normal routine.

Most of us are so busy and we've got so many things to think about, that we automate our responses.

Yes, we say "thank you" as we receive the coffee. But as soon as the cup is in our clutches, our eyes and attention are already moving on to the next task — where's the cream and sugar table? Where's the door? Where are my car keys?

So today we're going to un-automate our gratitude. Instead of doing this simple thing by rote, we're going to bring a vacation level of consciousness to our expressions of gratitude.

Say "thanks" like you really mean it. I know you do, of course. But when you say it, be present. Look at that person. Pause for a moment. Say thank you and really feel the gratitude.

Say it differently than normal. "Thanks" could become a more elaborate "Thank you. I really appreciate that."

Remember last week when you were on vacation, and you saw something new for the first time? Maybe it was that amazing sunset. The infinity pool. The quaint Italian village square.

When you saw something like that, you FELT a sense of appreciation. You loved that moment. I'm suggesting you bring *that* feeling to each moment today when you thank someone.

Take a vacation from your normal way of thanking people. Bring your vacation vibe to them.

There, you did it! Your first day *not* on vacation wasn't so bad, was it?

You eased yourself back into the swing of things. You reminded yourself to express appreciation for people in your life.

All in all, a good day back.

8

A VACATION FROM LIFE AS USUAL

Yesterday, your focus was to genuinely express gratitude to three people. What was that like? Did those three people respond to your kind gesture? And most importantly, was it good for you?

I joke about that, but there's a lot of truth in the question. Saying thank you to someone else, and really meaning it, isn't just good for the other person. It's good for you.

Could you tell the difference between your normal way of saying "thank you," and this more heightened approach? Most people say yes. It makes them feel better.

If you want to keep the good feelings going on this, your second day back from vacation, continue to express gratitude to people.

Today we're going to flash back to your second day of vacation. On that day, we focused on being mindful during our vacation experience.

We deliberately noticed and appreciated everything around us. Let's try the same thing today.

When you were on vacation, probably almost everything about the experience was new to you. The destination, the activities, the people, and part of that "newness" that makes a vacation so stimulating.

You're like a kid, where everything is new to you. Whatever you encounter delights and brings a smile to your face.

And then you return home. Where you know everything.

You get up in the morning and begin your day on autopilot. Maybe it looks like this:

- You could make your coffee with your eyes closed.
- Your car could drive itself to work, even if it's not a Tesla.
- Your Pandora app cranks out the same music presets.
- Your work or school routine is exactly that — routine.
- You exchange emails with the same people.
- You eat lunch in the same place.
- You leave the office and head home using the same route.
- You eat dinner from a limited menu of comfort foods.
- Finally, you settle in to catch up on your un-binged shows, when—

"Ohmygod, STOP!" you may be thinking, "I need a vacation from this!" Yes, you do. But not necessarily a vacation where you go somewhere. You just had one of those.

No, you need a vacation from how you look at your day.

- Instead of going through the motions, go through the movements.
- Instead of being on autopilot, take the wheel and steer some place new.
- Instead of accepting the same old presets, pick a new song, or even a new station.

In short, decide to experience today as if home was brand new to you.

TODAY'S FOCUS

Here are three things you could do today to change up your normal routine and view home in a new way.

319. **ONE NEW THING.** First, discover one new or different thing about where you live. Drive on a new street. Explore a neighborhood you've never been to before. Stop in a new shop. If you always go left at the top of the subway escalator, go right instead. Try having lunch in a new place. Order something different. If you bring your own food, mix it up, have something you normally wouldn't eat.

320. HOW'S YOUR DAY GOING? Second, talk to one new person. This should be easy. Just find one person you've never spoken to and say hello. Whether it's at school, work, the gym, or the store, find at least one person you've never spoken with before.

What will you say? Whatever you want! Start with hello. Maybe ask them how their day is going.

If you did nothing more than that, followed by a warm, "Have a good day," you will have fulfilled the objective.

If you feel moved to carry the conversation further, then be talkative! Remember all the questions you asked someone on vacation (#205–#218)? Use those as conversation starters.

321. BE DARING. BE NEW. Finally, try something new today. If you go to the gym and you always work on the same machines, pick a new one today. If there's a dinner recipe you've wanted to try, make it tonight. If you always watch the same shows, read the same online sites, or watch the same sports, pick something new.

The point with all of these is to break up your normal routine.

Be willing to experience your normal life as if you were on vacation. Live a little bit outside your comfort zone. Be daring. Be adventurous. And of course, you don't have to limit yourself to just doing this today.

What about tomorrow? You could be especially daring and do this all over again! If not, I've got you covered with a new focus for Day 3.

9
RECHARGE A VACATION HABIT

It's your third day back home. Did you unpack yet? Because today we're going back to your third day of vacation. Well, sorta.

The theme that particular day was recharging. So guess what the theme is for today? That's right! Recharging. See, you've still got it!

Remember your third day of vacation? There were 55 activities you could have chosen to renew or recharge yourself. Things like taking a walk, going for a swim, meditating, or napping.

If you did one or more of those activities, I'm curious. Did you continue past that one day? If not, here's your chance.

Why not decide to take something you did on vacation, renew that commitment today, and then do it for an entire week.

First a note. Be easy on yourself. Sometimes we pick something too hard to do consistently. As I said when you were on vacation, if you picked something like "Run 3 miles every day," that might be challenging to do every day. So pick something easy to do.

Start by choosing a new habit, maybe something you did on vacation, and do this one simple thing for one week.

You might be thinking to yourself, what if I wasn't successful with that habit on vacation?

Perhaps you chose one with the best of intentions, but then discovered it wasn't right for you, or now wasn't the best time to take that on.

If that's the case, you get to pick a new one that you can begin today.

Here are a few examples to consider:

HEALTH

- Floss daily
- Do five sit-ups or push-ups every day
- Walk for five minutes
- Do twenty jumping jacks
- Stretch by touching your toes (or as close as you can get)
- Wrack up a certain number of steps on your fitness tracker

PEACE OF MIND

- Meditate (or just quiet your mind) for three minutes
- Write down one thing you're grateful for
- Spend five minutes journaling about your day ahead
- Pick an inspiring book and read ten minutes a day

ORGANIZATION

- Make your bed
- Tidy up the kitchen after breakfast
- Spend five minutes clearing out your email inbox
- Clean your desk off at the end of the workday
- Arrange tomorrow's clothes night

As you can see, these are all simple things you can do daily.

In most of the examples, I suggested a minor time commitment, such as reading ten minutes a day. You might choose an even smaller commitment if you think it will help you get started.

The key is to pick an amount you KNOW you can do. Once you get started, you could do more, if motivated. But at the very least, you will have met your commitment and can feel good about that. Anything else is gravy.

TODAY'S FOCUS

322. HABIT FOR A WEEK. Start up with your existing habit from vacation if that still works for you (see #300 and #301.) Or, if you've come up with a new one that's fine too.

But at this point, commit to doing one thing for the next seven days. Remember, make it simple, make it easy to do, then commit to it.

If you keep a journal, or if you have your vacation guide, make a note every day when you perform that habit. Have a great day!

10

BE INTENTIONAL WITH RELATIONSHIPS

You probably have been home 3–4 days by the time you read this. You're re-acclimating to your daily routine, catching up on work, projects, calls, and emails that piled up during your travels.

The first days back from vacation can be crazy. Maybe you're just now finally catching up. If so, take a moment to breathe — go ahead, inhale now — and let me ask you a question:

Is there anything you are forgetting?

Anything that could use a little more attention?

And by the way, if you did inhale, please now exhale... Ahhh...

You know where you may want to re-focus? Your relationships! That is, your spouse, your family, and your friends.

Yes, in that initial post-vacation whirlwind most of us experience, we're occupied with "must-do" activities. There are things we have to do and thus, it's easy to take our relationships for granted.

Why not spend catch-up time with your spouse or significant other? You've both been going full speed since you got back. A night with just the two of you would be nice. A chance to slide back into vacay mode for an hour or two.

Trust me, I know all the reasons you resist this idea. Your to-do list is only half done. You're still trying to catch up. You've got so many things going on.

And besides, nobody is really clamoring for time sitting around the table. I mean, you just spent a week together.

You probably ate together morning, noon, and night. The "credit" for that ought to last for at least a week or two. Everyone will understand if we forgo dinner tonight, right? After all, we can catch up with each other on the weekend, right?

Or maybe your relationship guilt comes in the form of that friend who called to see how your trip was. You'd like to call them back. You really would. But you're swamped. Maybe you can just text them and say now's not a good time, 'Can we catch up next week or the week after?'

Do you see now how this works? There will ALWAYS be a reason you can't spend time with loved ones, friends, or family.

Your reasons will probably seem justified in this first week. But won't there always be some excuse? Yes, there will.

So it's up to you. If you're going to maintain the vibrancy of those relationships, you must choose to invest your time in those people.

TODAY'S FOCUS

323. INTENTIONAL RELATIONSHIPS. Pick someone in your life — your spouse, your family, a friend, or a co-worker — and spend time with them. Whatever works for you. Lunch. Dinner. A walk in the park, a swim in the pool. Play a game. Share pictures. Trade stories.

Bottom line, spend time with that person or those people. Enjoy the experience. Celebrate what's special about that relationship. Who knows, maybe you'll want to do that again next week?

11
MAKE MEMORIES AT HOME

On your second day back from vacation, we talked about looking around your environment and seeing it with fresh eyes. Of course, it's easy to do when we're on vacation. Everything is new and unique.

But back home…it's just so familiar. You have your routines. Your customs. Your habits. But what if you didn't?

Aside from your daily routine, have you thought about what makes your home life interesting or unique?

What if the place you live now was a world-renowned vacation destination? Actually, it may be, depending on where you live. You may live in or near a destination that people from all over the world visit. New York, Los Angeles, Washington, D.C., Miami, Toronto, Hawaii, or Vancouver.

If you live in a place like this, well done, tourists call your home their vacation paradise.

You may not live in a world-renowned metropolis or tourist mecca. But there are probably still interesting aspects to your home. History, customs, drinks, food, famous residents.

No matter where you live, there's something that other people would likely find interesting about your home.

When you were on vacation, the Chapter 5 activities centered around creating memories of your trip, whether it was in a journal, with photos, or through shopping for that perfect souvenir.

Today we're going to apply those same ideas to your hometown.

TODAY'S FOCUS

324. HOMETOWN MEMORIES. Discover something unique or interesting about your town and share it with someone. Basically, imagine your hometown as if it were a tourist haven and look for a souvenir or memento you can share.

If you live in a place like New York, obviously you'll have lots of options. Get a takeout menu or printed napkin from an interesting restaurant. Find a brochure for a well-known tourist attraction. Send them sand from Key West, a leaf from Central Park, or a cable car ticket from San Francisco.

If you live in a smaller locale, and you don't think your town has anything interesting, think again. No matter what, there's likely something that would interest others.

Maybe your town doesn't have its own key chains or postcards. That's fine. Take a picture, print it out, and mail that. What's the oldest building? What's the biggest park? Who's the most famous resident? Have fun with this!

Hopefully, this focus leads you to see your home in the same way you saw your vacation destination.

If you open your eyes to what's new and unique and think about sharing your experience with someone else, you may appreciate home in a whole new way.

12

DECIDE FOR YOUR FUTURE

This is Day Six since you've been home from your vacation. Our time together is reaching a conclusion. But your time with "you" is just beginning.

Most people go on vacation to escape from their normal life. I hope during this process you've discovered it's possible to create a life from which you don't want to escape.

You can be more connected to things, to people, and to yourself. You discovered this doesn't happen by accident. You didn't just sit by the pool drinking mai tais and your life got better all by itself. You took steps to make that happen.

You have the same choice now as you did then. Once you close this book, what choices will you make? What actions will you take?

You may be tempted to think it was easy to do all these things while you were on vacation. But now that you're back in reality, there's no way you could continue. But is that true? Think about it for a moment.

You had all the possible distractions in the world — scenery, great food, relaxation, family, sightseeing — yet you managed to do at least one meaningful thing each day.

Despite all the other things you could have done, you decided to do one or two things a day. So why not decide that you could continue to do one meaningful thing each day? Yes, you're not physically on vacation.

But what's stopping you from *mentally* being on vacation?

Don't get me wrong. I'm not suggesting you go to work in flip-flops, a drink in hand, vibing Jimmy Buffet as you zone out. Not at all.

But you get to choose how you go through your day. You get to choose the attitude you leave the house with. You can decide which version of you meets with people. You can decide how you'll respond to challenges.

You can live your life with gratitude, a sense of discovery, and a new commitment to the people you love. You can make every day unique and memorable. And you can make your life experience as joyous, fulfilling, and impactful as you choose it to be.

How do you do this?

Start with a decision. Decide right now — or in two hours, if that's more convenient. But really, now is WAY better — decide that the next time you go on vacation, you will be a changed person.

You will have continued this process of growth, and the version of you that travels next time will be different as a result.

If we were taking the classic "before" and "after" pictures, you'd see the difference, even in a small way. Honestly, you don't have to go from twig thin to Dwayne Johnson. But decide you will continue these processes, so the next time you go away, you will be a little bit happier, stronger, more grateful, more connected, more true to the best version of you that's possible.

Decide you will go on vacation not to escape from you, but to celebrate and appreciate you. Decide that taking time off isn't to recover, but to explore, renew, and recommit.

Once you've made this decision, you might be thinking, how do you do this? Find a new book that intrigues you and work through that. Listen to inspiring podcasts. Attend lectures. Watch YouTube videos that enlighten you.

You could also start with this book, which you already have. Pick up the book (or e-reader, if that's how you're reading it), flip through the pages, then stop on one randomly. Scan the page and find an exercise. Do that one. Or the one next to it. Whichever.

Just choose something, and then do that today. Almost every single one of the 325 suggestions in this book could be done at home. You don't have to go on vacation again to live this life.

You might also find that this process causes you to get a better idea. Go with that. Your higher power intuitively knows exactly what's best for you. Follow that.

Maybe the exercise you pick that day doesn't feel right or possible. But you instantly have an idea of how to do it differently. Follow that. Do it. Then do this for the next 365 days.

Try to get better each day, even just a little bit, and I promise you the version of you that travels next will be incredibly grateful for the decisions and actions that "present you" takes today.

TODAY'S FOCUS

325. "DEAR ME..." Write yourself a letter, to be sent to you in six months (or whatever would be a likely midpoint between now and the next time you take a vacation.) In this letter, tell yourself about the decision you've made today. Describe what this mindful vacation process has meant to you. Tell your "future self" one simple thing you are committed to doing. And close by recommitting to your own personal growth before your next vacation.

This message to your future self can either be a real written letter, or an email. If by mail, ask someone you trust to send it at the appropriate date. If by email, you can use a service like www.futureme.org, which allows you to write a private email which they'll deliver at the date of your choosing.

However you decide to send the letter, be sure to write it. Your totally awesome future vacation self will thank you.

AFTERWORD

Wow! You're done! You finished *Best Vacation Ever*. Hopefully your experience reading the book matched the title. Please know I have loved being on this journey with you.

As I wrote this book, I tried to imagine you, the reader, allowing me the honor of spending your precious vacation time reading this book. I imagined the book at the beach, on ships, and in foreign countries. I imagined that every week of the year, I would vicariously go on vacation somewhere in the world. So I thank you for that privilege.

Please drop me a line (I'm @thorchallgren on social media) and let me know what this experience has meant to you, and where in the world we traveled.

Until the next vacation we spend together, I wish you a happy life, and happy traveling.

Thor

QUICK START IDEAS

Want to quickly dive into vacay mode? Try these quick start ideas. Choices in **BOLD** are top picks.

CHAPTER 1: **#1**, **#7**, #8, **#18**, #22, and #34.

CHAPTER 2: **#64**, #71, #73, **#81**, #87, #90, #94, and **#109**.

CHAPTER 3: **#112**, #118, **#127**, #129, **#134**, #143, #148, and **#155**.

CHAPTER 4: **#166**, #177, #180, #184, **#196**, **#205**, #210, and #214.

CHAPTER 5: #227, **#230**, #234, #245, **#255**, **#256**, #281, and #287.

CHAPTER 6: **#290**, #294, #299, **#300**, #305, and **#314**.

For **COUPLES** traveling together, explore this list of activities.

#22 A HALLMARK MOMENT
#115 KIDS LOVE TO FLOAT
#131 SLIP INTO THE TUB
#133 "KIDS, WE'RE GETTING A SITTER"
#177 GETTING TO KNOW YOU
#178 WHERE TO NEXT?
#179 LET'S MOVE HERE!
#180 IT'S YOURS!

#181 HELLO, I'M...
#182 THE INTERVIEW
#183 IF YOU COULD STAY ANYWHERE
#185 WRITE IT DOWN
#186 COMPARED TO HOME
#195 GO ON A DATE
#197 PLAY GAMES
#305 SEVEN DAYS FROM NOW

If you're traveling with kids, here's an entire list of 53 family-friendly, kid approved activities.

#21 WHAT I LIKE ABOUT YOU
#24 DEAR MOMMY OR DADDY
#28 LEAVE A NOTE
#31 THANK YOU ARTWORK
#35 HELPFUL KIDS
#37 AND THE AWARD GOES TO...
#48 PRAISE BE VACATION
#49 RISE ABOVE!
#59 EXTRA! EXTRA!
#62 SUMMER SCHOOL
#67 KIDS' TURN
#69 THE KIDS' POV
#74 WHAT'S THE OLDEST THING?
#75 CHILDLIKE WONDER
#96 KIDS! EAT DESSERT FIRST!
#110 KIDS SHARE THE DARNDEST THINGS
#115 KIDS LOVE TO FLOAT!
#128 BARTER WITH THE KIDS
#133 "KIDS, WE'RE GETTING A SITTER"
#140 "KIDS, LET'S PLAY A GAME"
#151 PLAY OUTDOORS WITH THE KIDDOS
#170 THE STORY OF ME
#173 JUST A TYPICAL DAY
#175 TO DREAM THE IMPOSSIBLE DREAM
#179 LET'S MOVE HERE!
#183 IF YOU COULD STAY ANYWHERE...
#185 WRITE IT DOWN

#186 COMPARED TO HOME
#188 THAT PERSON IS...INTERESTING
#189 DISNEY WORLD FOREVER!
#190 WOULD MOM AND DAD GO WITH YOU?
#192 TELL ME MORE...
#194 WHEN I WAS YOUR AGE
#195 GO ON A DATE
#196 GO ON A PICNIC
#197 PLAY GAMES
#200 BACK TO SCHOOL
#201 GAME NIGHT!
#202 GET COOKING!
#217 ONE NEW FRIEND A DAY
#224 SHARE PHOTOS
#230 BEST PICTURES EVER
#245 SILLY PICTURES
#246 SILLY PICTURE CONTEST
#255 START WITH A LIST
#256 LET THE KIDS SHOP TOO
#273 WHAT WILL I WRITE ABOUT?
#276 HIT THE "RECORD" BUTTON
#279 CREATE ART
#283 WE WERE HERE
#297 THE KIDS ARE MOVING HERE!
#301 MAKE IT RIDICULOUS
#305 SEVEN DAYS FROM NOW

ACKNOWLEDGMENTS

In order to write a book, it takes a TON of people who supported the effort. Since this is a book about vacations, I actually feels like these people went with me on an actual vacation! Looking at it that way, I think this book should qualify for some kind of Guiness Record for largest group vacation. Maybe? On to the thanks...

First, to my Team Book Launch, thanks for being my first readers and champions. To Shirin, Tracy, Natasha, Gary, Karena, Lisa D, Debbie, Lisa G, Joan, Janis and Katie, I appreciate you all SOO much!!

To those on Team Thor, I'm greatly indebted to the friends and family who encouraged and supported me on this journey. To Dr. James Mellon, for the "Action!"-taking prompt that got this book over the hurdle.

Thanks to Tiffany Carter the positive no-nonsense advice. To Chandler Bolt, who simplified the book writing process. To Rob Murgatroyd, the first guest on my podcast, whose praise at that stage meant the world to me, grazie mille!

Many thanks also to Lisa Rule and Jim Rule at the Acorn Newspapers, who were the first people to say "yes" to my idea of writing about travel. To my newspaper editor Kyle Jorrey, who read at least 100,000+ words in my columns, and supported me along the way, thank you!

To my longtime friends Mark Wolfe and Jane Wolfe, who patiently listened to all the things I said I would do one now, and never appeared to doubt it was possible, I appreciate all your support.

Thanks to my longtime friends in the travel industry: Pauline Pancake, Linda Halstead, DC Milic Vekic, Dave Fowlie, and so many others to which I'm grateful for your friendship on my travel journeys.

Finally, I want to express my love and gratitude to my daughter Sara and my wife Erin. Sara would often receive texts from me asking for feedback on this or that. I was always thrilled when she liked something. Thank you! Erin has been a dream spouse for someone writing a book. Her feedback is sound and honest. Her encouragement sustained me on this long journey. And her support in giving me the space to do this means everything.

AUTHOR

Thor Challgren is a travel industry veteran and author of 150+ newspaper columns on travel. Thor loves adventuring to new destinations as well as sipping pina coladas at swim-up bars. He is certified with the Life Mastery Institute, and loves helping people discover their purpose at thorchallgren.com. Thor holds an MFA in writing from UCLA and lives in Southern California with his wife.

Connect with Thor on social media:

READER BONUS

To start your vacation STRESS-FREE, get my FREE checklist planner, which you can download at bestvacationeverbook.com.

If you want to share this book with others, but you absolutely want to keep YOUR copy, tell them to get their own. Be nice, of course, after all, you're on vacation. Nicely tell them they can use their smartphone to scan this QR code, which will whisk them to the book order page.

Made in the USA
Las Vegas, NV
24 May 2022